ALL
ACCESS

An event professionals guide to
getting the respect, promotion,
and salary they deserve.

Christina Zara, CMP, CMM

Pig N Peacock Publishing

All Access: An event professional's guide to getting the respect, promotion, and salary they deserve.

Published by Gatekeeper Press

2167 Stringtown Rd, Suite 109

Columbus, OH 43123-2989

www.GatekeeperPress.com

The cover design and editorial work for this book are entirely the product of the author. Gatekeeper Press did not participate in and is not responsible for any aspect of these elements.

FIRST EDITION

Cover design by: Mark Ruckey

Copy Editing by: Michelle Edwards

ISBN (paperback): 9781662920585

eISBN: 9781662920592

Dedication

This book is dedicated to

my many coaches and mentors who held me accountable

the colleagues, family, and friends who held my heart

to Chris who held my hair

and to my husband, who held my hand…

through it all.

TABLE OF CONTENTS

ACKNOWLEDGEMENTS:

First and foremost, special thanks to my biggest cheerleader and best friend Jonathan Zara. I am so lucky to have you walk this crazy, chaotic, and ridiculously entertaining journey with me. I love your more than I can say and I couldn't have asked for a better partner in this life. I love you so much, so much, so much. 😊

Thanks to my mother and father who taught me at an early age to live my own life. Who told me that it's ok to be yourself and live each day with the realization that tomorrow is promised to no one, so you better make this life count!

To my big brother Rich who ate my vegetables as a kid and taught me how to fight the right way. Thanks for having my back all these years. No matter what I know you are just a phone call away and that means the world to me.

Chris Williams and Dave Watson, thank you for being members of my family. Your undying encouragement and support mean so much to me. Thank you both for being a consummate light in my life that always knows right when to shine its brightest. Chris, you know I love you more and since this is now in print forever, I suppose that means I win.

Special thanks to my fellow El Diablo Mark. You are not only a superb travel companion, but you are also my brother. I have so much to thank you for that I couldn't possibly fit it all here. Just know that I value our friendship and I love you deeply.

To Jacquie who embraced the little event planner from Georgia. Thank you for opening your arms and bringing me into the Florida culture. Thanks to you I am comfortable wearing flip-flops to the grocery store and jean shorts to the "fancy" places. I'm so looking forward to many more times together.

JP, thank you for your generosity and friendship, for always picking up the phone when I call, and for your undying positivity. I love you my brother from another mother, and I will always have your back.

Cyndi Plamondon who is a true leader in every sense of the word. Thank you for putting your staff first, your emotions second, and leading by example. I will always remember our cheeseburger business meetings and how much you taught me about holding your head high especially through adverse situations. You are a true lady.

Thank you to Carol Jones who gave me the confidence to chase my dreams. I will always treasure your friendship.

Special thank you to Michelle Springer my first editor and cousin from Boston. Thank you for keeping it real and driving my vision in a positive direction. You are a big reason I fulfilled my commitment, and I will always be grateful.

Tabe for being my therapist when I need it. Cannot thank you enough for introducing us to aggravation and all the great times spent in your company working on "snugging" my players.

Thank you to "The Originals" who taught me more about being a leader, mentor, and more importantly friend. I hold you all in a very special place in my heart. It is the place where we are forever playing murder in the dark, where we are the first ones on the dance floor, and we play "sweet child" at inappropriate times. I owe so much to each of you individually but thank you all for being so "sweat".

To "Simple Mike" Jaros who promoted me in title and support. Although we didn't hire Weezer, you were the best boss a girl like me could hope for. Thank you for knowing and exercising the true meaning of leadership.

A special thank you to Patti Johnson and Jeff Berger. You both gave me some solid advice and mentorship through the years. You are both very special people to so many professionals. I admire you for so many things and appreciate your friendship more than you know.

To Chuck Tallent and the brilliant crew of Gray Matter Productions. "We did the things." Some of the best days of my life were spent in your company, and I couldn't have asked for a better partner. Thank you for keeping me grounded and dreaming all at the same time. No matter where this life takes us, I will always remember you fondly.

Thank you so much to my work Army and friends at the Academy. You have all embraced me so quickly and I am constantly impressed with your passion and work ethic.

To my friend and mentor Pete Scott, thank you so much for giving me the freedom to chase my dream and the support to carry it through. You are a great man respected by many and truly deserving of all rewards life bestows upon you.

A huge thank you to my event professional family who shared their stories and allowed me to use them in this book. I'm grateful to each of you for so many things.

Thank you mostly to anyone who has chosen event planning as a carrier. I highly respect and value all of you. I just know in my heart that one day we will obtain our rightful seat at the executive table throughout all businesses and industries.

Let's do this.

FOREWORD:

As someone who works in both the meetings and events world, and personal and professional development, this book hits home for me.

Christina and I met in a somewhat random, but actually logical way. When Meeting Professionals International (MPI) offered it's first CMP at Sea program in January 2020, I was asked to teach, and Christina decided to register.... even though she had her CMP already. At that I knew I respected her, even though we had not met. Anyone who has a CMP and CMM and still comes to education that others might say "I don't need that" ---is my type of person.

As I read this book, I learned far more about Christina's career than I knew before. I knew she had held some very high positions, and as I mentioned before she was "doubly credentialed". What I did not know was how she got there.

In the meetings and events industry, one of the interesting things to observe is how people think of career growth, really depends on when they came into the industry—not what age but when. In the past 50 years there has been an evolution of the role of a Planner, so depending on what decade you started---your story is different. At least in some ways.

As you read the book you will see what changes...and what doesn't. And why things that are accepted, are not necessarily acceptable. Especially if you want to move your career forward and be seen as something more than an "order taker", or to use a very old derogatory term, a "coffee cup counter".

Not that this is a history of Meeting and Event Planning. This is a living, breathing document, that is applicable to your career no matter how old you are and what stage you are in. It's about having a mindset, vision, and using the wisdom Christina shares, based on her experience and others she has known.

It is from the heart and at times it will hit you in the gut. It will make you laugh… and cry, with both disbeliefs, and finding out you are not the only one who has these things happen.

So yes, it's a little bit history, a little bit storytelling, but most importantly, it is a very readable step by step guide as to what to do to legitimately get the respect you deserve. I am fond of saying that our stakeholders tend to take the attitude of "How hard can it be to get a room and order some coffee?" My answer: Much harder than you think if you are doing it right.

This is a good, comfortable read, packed with information you can use immediately.

I know Christina and I are both watching to see where you go,

Joanne Dennison, MSEd, CMP

The MeetGuide

Guiding you through the world of Meeting and Events

The Guidance Counselor for Grown Ups

Working with individuals and organizations to answer "What's Next?"

Introduction

Despite being critical to the success of any organization, event professionals continue to be locked out of the C-suite. We know full well our worth, our contribution, and our role. The problem is C-suite leaders do not. As we struggle to be heard and help our leadership avoid common industry mistakes and expensive pitfalls, our daily efforts can feel more like a battle than a workday. When event decisions are made behind closed doors, our work will continue to be negatively impacted and our professional glass ceiling will remain impregnable.

I have worked as an event professional for more than twenty years. During this time, I have developed a passion for this industry and the event professionals who have chosen this carrier path. I have seen a lot during my tenure and come to the decision event professionals are some of the hardest working, overlooked professionals in any setting. This line of work is highly misunderstood, highly stressful, and disproportionally rewarded.

Despite the odds, I have enjoyed numerous successes throughout my career, including receiving leadership awards, professional accolades, industry acknowledgement, and the highest possible position for an event professional: having complete autonomy over an event department and program.

If you are considering a career as an event professional, having your own event business, or are looking to advance to C-suite status within your organization, then this book is for you.

Though my personal journey and hilariously unbelievable stories, we will explore the candid issues facing our profession today, expose industry myths, and examine the ridiculous demands put upon us. In the end I will equip you with the necessary tools to propel you to the C-suite, become an industry advocate, and a beacon of admiration for the next generation of event professionals. If you are ready to turn a job you love into a career you can be proud of, then start reading today.

Chapter 1: How did we get here?

To change our future, we must look to the past to fully understand how we arrived here.

Imagine, if you will, a dark office building circa 1973. The carpet is thick and orange, the air heavy with the faint smell of cigarette smoke. A secretary is dressed in a grey, heavy wool suit. Clacking away on a vintage typewriter, she scribes her boss's words from an old dictation machine. The clicking sound of the typewriter seems to harmonize with the percolating coffee machine, ringing desk phones, and the whispered office gossip by the water cooler.

A heavy, wooden door separating the secretary's desk from her boss's rather large office suddenly swings open and a large, balding man exits. He removes a wet smoldering cigar from his lips and gruffly announces, "I would like to host a client gathering this Friday."

The secretary, already knowing the expectation of her, reaches for her pad and pencil. The man wastes no time conveying the details. He prattles on, relaying the guest list, expectations for the food and beverage, and then added, "I expect this gathering to be an affair that will dazzle my guests."

Then, without bothering to ask if she has any follow-up questions, he turns and disappears back into his office. She glances at her desktop calendar. It is Monday afternoon. Despite already working on a rather large project, she now needs to find the time and resources to plan the client party for this coming Friday. She will also need to adjust her plans and find a sitter to watch her children for that evening.

Not given time to complain, she goes to work outlining all the tasks required to manage the client cocktail party. She calls the guests (as there is no time for paper invitations), works with the local liquor store to deliver drinks, and asks a friend to bartend. She gets her cousin, who works in the kitchen of a local inn, to help with catering.

Despite the growing number of questions she has for the boss, he replies to her inquiries with the same phrase, "I'm sure you will figure it out." She does her best, all the while struggling to keep up with her daily workload, which is admittedly suffering due to the added demand of the party.

Fast forward to the big day. The rented tables are dressed in fine linen, the votive candles lit, and crystal glasses and cubed ice at the ready for cocktails. The secretary, standing in the room reviewing her work, takes a moment to silently congratulate herself on a job well done before the first guest arrives and she calls to check in with her babysitter.

The occasion goes well, even better than she expected. Her typically grumpy boss even seems pleased and is chatting with a few key clients near the bar. At the event's end, she cleans the now empty area with a smile on her face, satisfied with her work. She pays the vendors, locks up the office, and heads home feeling a sense of pride.

Monday morning, she is gleefully brewing a pot of coffee and anticipating her boss's appreciation. She enters his large, wood-panel office and places a hot cup of coffee on his desk. He accepts the cup, takes a deep sip, and sits back in his chair before removing his reading glasses to address her.

"I can't understand why the dictation project I gave you last week isn't complete," he states dryly. She feels her heart fall into her pumps.

"Didn't I give that to you on Monday?" She is too stunned to reply as he continues to lecture her on how disappointed he is it has taken her so long to complete it and goes so far as to question her typing skills.

When he finishes the reprimand, she turns on her heel exiting the office and closing the heavy wooden door behind her. Tears already welling in her eyes, she seeks comfort in her chair. Finding a tissue in her purse, she allows herself to daydream of her boss choking on his morning coffee. She gleefully envisions him gagging in agony, clutching his neck and gasping for air like a freshly caught fish before she takes a deep breath and gets to work on completing the dictation project. Yes, the very project he interrupted a week ago with a demand to plan the client event.

Sadly, this was not the last time she was asked out of the blue to organize his client gatherings. Before her retirement in the late 1980s, she worked in tortured silence as she was even asked to plan eventually his personal gatherings from his wedding anniversary to his children's graduation parties.

What you just read is the true story of my aunt Rainy. Her story may sound familiar to some of you even today, minus the cigars and ashtrays, of course. It's not uncommon for us to be in the middle of a project requiring complete concentration only to be interrupted to focus on what leadership deems important. Embedded deep into the fabric of this story is a key reason event professionals are overlooked for a seat at the table.

The 1970s were by no means the beginning of our industry but rather a blip. We could argue our profession even traces back to the beginning of man. Yes, the very beginning. I'm talking Cro-Magnon. Before there was language, the written word, and agendas, man survived. Can't imagine that was easy living, but they figured it out. They knew when the weather changed, they would need to more food, so they figured out how to track prey, cook, and use animal materials to make clothes, shelter, and tools.

As early man evolved, so did our industry. Think about it - someone had to step up and organize their way of life for survival. They had to make a plan, organize the hunts, figure out a food-based budget that included how much the tribe would need to survive the long winters. They even created the world's first whiteboard when they scribbled plans on the cave walls. Historians agree, in addition to being decorative, cave art was used by man to convey the best way to kill a beast or warn others of what lay in the terrain. This organized documentation is the very start of many professions, ours being among them.

The early man figured out the imperative need for organization. To strategize a plan of how to achieve a task on or before a specific date. The key to their very survival was the planner in the tribe who figured it out.

Let us hop forward a few millennia. I mean, cavemen are one thing but consider a more modern world. Meeting

Professional International (MPI)'s tagline is, "When we meet, we change the world." How true is that? Consider some of the most iconic events in history. Maybe you are thinking of the signing of the Constitution, or the first Olympic Games in Greece, or perhaps the historic and moving March on Washington rally that championed the iconic "I Have a Dream" speech delivered by Dr. Martin Luther King, Jr.

Event professionals were critical to all of these events. Take the signing of the Constitution: someone had to select the date and time and communicate to those signing, plus even handle little details like having enough ink in the quill to complete the task.

The first Olympic Games in Greece happened in 776 B.C. Did that just "come together"? Uh, no! Someone had to decide which events would happen when, invite neighboring towns to compete, plan for housing of traveling athletes and the male members of their families (about 40,000 people), plan the parade, and keep the women out (look it up).

Don't even get me started on how they marketed the event. Remember this was pre-printing press, so my closest guess is a group of traveling "invitations" who stood in town squares shouting, "Lend me your ear, men. For you are invited to Greece to watch other men compete in some serious man-on-man trials. In the end, one alpha man will be crowned with some olive leaves because we think Zeus would like that kind of thing."

I'm about 95 percent positive that is how the invitation sounded, but don't quote me on that.

Back to our history, the March on Washington, DC, in 1963 was organized by Phillip Randolph and Bayard Rustin and attracted somewhere between 200,000 – 300,000 attendees. It included an organized lineup of speakers, specific content, and a massive audio-visual package, which allowed everyone in attendance to hear the presentations. The time and effort put in by these two gentlemen is astonishing and worth looking up. I especially enjoyed how they selected the venue.

But, unlike Mr. Randolph and Mr. Rustin, the person with the idea to hold the event rarely puts in the effort to plan it. I'm guessing it was the ruler of Olympia who one day, while sitting about being fanned by palm fronds and fed grapes, said, "Hey, hold up! Don't you guys think it would be cool if we held a *mano a mano* competition to please Zeus?" Then after gaining consensus, he most likely micro-managed the work of the planning crew up and through the full event. Ah, the humble beginnings of the stakeholder.

But seriously, think for a moment of all the work that went into these historical events and so many more. Imagine if everyone had a rotten time at the first Olympic Games. How would history have changed if, say, they were rained out or the competitions didn't delight the audiences? Well, the odds are the tradition of the Olympics probably wouldn't have lived on until today. Is it not an argument then that planners have been darn important since the beginning of time?

If you are like me, you like gross stuff. The more grotesque the better, so to further illustrate our importance throughout history, I have selected an event to dissect the planner's role and how, without us, history could have been very different.

It starts with a banquet. The year is 1440 AD. James II is King of Scotland. His advisors fear the growing popularity of the Douglas clan and have worked themselves into a frenzy convincing themselves the young Earl of Douglas, both handsome and well spoken, will most certainly revolt against the crown and claim it as his own.

There is no real evidence of this, of course, only the fear of the Earl's increasing popularity and thought of possibly losing their powerful, cushy jobs. Instead of approaching the situation with any real logic, they convince themselves the clan is up to no good and needs to be stopped immediately. Contributing to this belief is the age of the King. James II is about ten years old and therefore vulnerable.

So, the young King's advisers do what any levelheaded, wilted, power-hungry man of that era would do. They devise a plan to host a dinner, invite the young Earl of Douglas, seize him, and murder him. Erasing the threat and allowing them to sleep peacefully at night. So, off they went to set the plan in motion.

First order of business, they tell ten-year-old King James II they think it would be a great idea for him to hold a gala dinner for the prominent Earl of Douglas to strengthen his relationship with the crown. The King thinks it is a jolly idea, so now a well-crafted invitation to the Earl of Douglas is sent out reading 'Come eat, enjoy, and then die, you scum.'

Ok, you got me, it didn't. But the advisors didn't have to work too hard to get the Earl to agree to the dinner due to a nasty rumor circulating that perhaps the handsome Earl wasn't the true son of his less than attractive father.

He had a lot to lose if this rumor took any real form, so he figured a sit down with the King, who had the power to dispel the hearsay, was probably worth his while. Hence, he gleefully accepts the invite and notes he will bring along his younger brother David as his plus one. When word of his acceptance reaches the castle, there is much celebration: "Yay, let the murdering commence!"

Fast forward to the night of the dinner. King James II and the Earl are getting along quite nicely. It's obvious that the young King is enjoying his company, and they are talking, laughing, and having a grand ole time right up to the point when the Earl is delivered a bloody entrée of the severed black bullhead. Pretty sure that's not what he ordered because, back in 1440, if you were served the severed head of a black bull, it meant you were about to die.

I warned you this would be pretty gruesome. So, there he is with a plate of sticky, bloody severed black bullhead. Imagine his thoughts before he and poor little David were seized and taken out back for a very quick and, dare I say, rigged trial. Both were found guilty of high treason and beheaded right there, right then, and on the spot.

Now, you may be asking yourself, why would you walk me down such a gruesome story in history? It's so I can further illustrate the important role the event planners played here. Let's break it down. The brains behind the organization of the dinner are credited to Sir William Crichton. Now there was a professional planner! He oversaw the creation of the friendly invitation, planned the menu, organized the seating chart, drew up the banquet event order, and added the idea of the severed bullhead for a bit of dramatic flair.

Also consider he had the forethought to remove the Earl and his brother outside for the trial knowing they would be executed, thus considering the difficulty of cleaning up the mess.

Had they just tried and murdered them in the royal dining hall, well who knows how long that cleanup would take and would they even finish in time for breakfast service the following morning? Sir William planned all of this without even a hint of danger reaching the young Earl or his kin.

Imagine all the work Sir William had on the day of the gala. He greeted the guests, showing them to their accommodations, and probably came to fetch them for dinner because you know he wanted to keep a close eye on them. He more than likely queued the band to play some fun, uplifting music, maybe organized a dancer or two to perform for the occasion. All the while, he was probably searching for the judge and the lawyers and wondering when the executioner was going to show. Had he remembered to tell him he would be beheading two people that day? Had he paid all the vendors?

Imagine Sir William as the festivities ensued, watching for social cues and picking the perfect time to signal servants to serve the bull's head. Then taking control of the room, ordering for the Earl and his brother to be seized and removed to the courtyard for the trial is to unfold.

Once he sees to it they are both quite dead, he most likely says a speech and a quick prayer for their souls. Then after ordering the staff to begin the cleanup, aids in consoling the King, who, it is recorded, was visibly upset to see his new bestie lose his head. Had Sir William done a shoddy job, it's possible the Douglas brothers may have had a clue and not only escaped the outcome but made good on the perceived threat of attack.

If you think about it, Sir William proved to be an amazing event professional and the success of the event should be credited directly to his skills. But I'll bet his reward, in addition to his satisfaction of a job well done, was to stay to oversee the cleanup as well as begin to plan for any retaliation that would be brought upon them from the Douglas clan. Our work is truly never done.

We understand our importance and the difference we make today, but a large reason we are locked out of the C-suite lay within history, so I have one final history lesson to provide some clarity. Arguably the most industry-defining age for event planners lay within the Edwardian era. This time in history was a pinnacle example of the have and have nots. The class system was so rigidly defined, the effects continue to bleed into modern-day society and, as mentioned, are one of the main reasons our profession is still viewed as a "downstairs" position.

One of my favorite TV series is PBS's *Manor House*. Anyone who knows me has heard me discuss this program, probably at length. The program is commonly described as a fascinating look at the grand British class system of the early 1900s. It is a social experiment to ascertain how modern-day people would cope with the upstairs/downstairs roles of an authentically recreated manor house from the early twentieth century.

A family of four was given the identity of turn-of-the-century aristocrats and fifteen people, considered successful in their walk through life, were given the identities as below-stairs house servants. À la *Downton Abbey*. The participants embodied their identities for three months, exposing the lives of the have and have nots in a way that remains with me since I watched the program in 2002.

To best illustrate my point on how this period-in-time directly contributes to our roles within organizations today, we skip to episode five of the series. Events are being organized at the manor house to celebrate the British Empire's colonial prowess and success. Stop there. Events are being organized, so let's examine what that looks like. It starts, like so many events do, by the ringing of a bell by the lady of the house as she summons her head maid and begins to dictate her thoughts on throwing a grand gala.

Feverishly, the head maid jots down all the desires while asking a few questions to ensure she has the demands correct. Then, at the staff dinner that evening, the she announces to the below-stairs servants the grand party is to take place in two weeks. As she reads the list of demands, the camera does a brilliant job capturing the downstairs crew's faces, giving away their true thoughts.

They do not envision happy guests as the lady of the house did. No, they see something entirely different; all they see is logistics. They are already pondering how in the hell they are going to pull this off with equipment like wood-burning stoves, ice-block refrigerators, heavy pottery for plates, cloth napkins, and the countless number of steps they will take from kitchen to yard and yard to kitchen to serve warm food and cold drinks.

On top of that, the head maid announced the requirement of live music, fireworks, and party games. Despite their reservations, of which there were many, the team went to work. They brainstormed ideas for the menu, drinks, games, invitations, and timing. Sound familiar?

The days leading up to the event were hectic, to say the least. In addition to working their normal manor duties, the staff often labored well into the evening hours to make the proper arrangements necessary for the event.

Two long weeks of physical and emotional distress did pay off in the end, as the exhausted staff came together to throw a hell of an epic party.

It was a beautiful day to hold the party, the lawn freshly cut and not a cloud in the sky. The staff small but mighty came together to help one another out, making sure each had a short break here and there throughout the day to avoid heat exhaustion and fatigue.

The guests enjoyed the party games, clay shooting, and at the end of the evening were pleasantly surprised to see the handmade firework display.

Again, the crew at PBS did a perfect job of capturing the staff's struggle against the leisure activities of the top family and guests. When the evening ended, many of the staff led guests to the exit, sweat pouring off their faces and forcing a smile through the exhaustion they felt. When the last guest made their way to the exit, the crew gathered around the staff dining room table congratulating each other on a job well done, rubbing their feet, and toasting wine, and expressing joy and relief that it was finally over.

Upstairs the top cast positioned themselves in a sort of reception line making sure they were able to properly say goodbye to everyone who attended. As the guests made their way along the line, each one expressed how impressed they were with the outcome and what a grand time they had. Several attendees mentioned how in awe they were that something of this size could have been pulled off given the lack of modern conveniences.

The upstairs family smiled, shook hands, and thanked their guests. Then they retired to the drawing room to congratulate each other on a job well done.

The staff cleaned the dishes, removed debris from the yard, gathered any remaining trash, and prepared for the following day. Meanwhile, the lady of the house was having her hair brushed and braided for bed, she shared her thoughts on the event. First, she commented how tired she was due to the events of the day. But then looking straight into the camera said the following, "I simply love throwing parties here, they are no trouble at all."

I leave you with that for a moment.

Can you see the similarities? How our role hasn't evolved that much from this Edwardian era? They do say that history repeats itself, and I suppose to some extent they are right. Even today we do our jobs so easily, so effortlessly leadership often does not see or realize the difficult work that goes into any successful event.

How often do we rub our sore feet, counting down the minutes before we get to lie in bed as they pat themselves on the back saying, "I just love putting on events, they are just no trouble at all"?

This episode left me with a thought I have not been able to shake since watching it for the first time, and it is that "This type of hierarchy still exists today." Decades have passed, and our industry, job duties, and professionalism continue to expand, so why are we sometimes still treated as the downstairs position, not worthy of growth? Well, let's get into that now.

Chapter 2: Portrait of the modern-day event professional

Welcome to the modern-day, and our industry has made some progress in gaining recognition. Our skill set is starting to see appropriate job titles and descriptions, and the line between executive administrators and event professionals is thinning. But the truth remains it is hard to gauge just how many event professionals there are practicing today.

So how many of us are there? Well, that is where our modern-day portrait gets sticky; see, it is hard to get a good count when your profession can't be tracked. What do I mean? Well, first there are too many titles associated with our job. There is the event planner, coordinator, manager, specialist, manager of meetings, manager of events, manager of meetings and events, tradeshow specialist, and the list goes on.

Also, you probably have had the fun experience of trying to select your profession from a website drop down menu only to settle for something like marketing, public relations, or hospitality professional. This is truly perplexing as we were awarded a Standard Industrial Classification (SIC) code in 2015 thanks to the hard work and effort put in by Janet Sperstad, CMP. So how come our code isn't widely used? It is clear, more than ever, we are a viable part of the company and, in many respects, more valued than ever before. But the truth is, we still have a long way to go.

Another major issue is who we report to. This one truly baffles me. More often than not, the event staff is tucked away under a completely obscure department and reports to someone with little to no event experience. The farther we are from C-suite executives, the less clear our contributions, successes, and workload become to that level, this makes it very easy to be overlooked as a viable position.

Chances are you are in this situation and your team either reports into either human resources or marketing. Isn't it a little odd that the head of the human resources department is a human resource professional, the head of marketing is a marketing professional, as is the same with Information Technology, Training, etc.? So how come event professionals end up reporting into one of these existing departments? How is it not its own stand-alone department with a department head who is an event professional? It is truly perplexing.

During my tenure as a professional, I have heard statements like: "Wow, I had no idea what went into making this happen," and "I'd promote you, but I really don't think we need a director of events." Why? Why not? Well, I have the answer. It all boils down to perception and knowledge.

Perception is that we have a fun, sexy job anyone's sibling or best friend can do because all event professionals are bubbly people pleasers who love to throw and attend parties. Knowledge is the unknown level of skill needed to be a truly creative, quality, time-saving, and money-saving event professional.

Both must be changed for us to stop fielding situations like this one that happened to me only a couple of years ago. A true story about competing perceptions. I was so proud of my promotion to manager of events. I was given a decent raise and an office. I started to feel like a professional, and I was excited for what my future held.

It was the third and final day of a leadership meeting held in San Francisco. The 250 leaders who were brought to the destination were running on their last fumes. You know the crowd, the ones who have been attending general sessions and breakouts for several days and are "networking" in the hotel lobby bar up to the wee hours of the night.

Despite my conversations with leadership warning them about attendee mental exhaustion and the rules to adult learning, they overworked the group. Leadership insisted that their message was so important they were going to work them to the last minute of the event. So, here we were on our last day, sitting in a dark room as executive after executive took the stage to gabble on about numbers in a monotone voice. You got it, a real yawn fest.

So, it was no shock that, when we took our first break, the attendees were none too motivated to head back inside when the xylophone chimed signaling for a return to the general session. Few moved back, while the majority just ignored the call and continued with what they were doing.

Then, through the crowd, I could see him approaching. The senior VP of sales, my boss's boss, was bolting right toward me. A tall older man who gave the impression he spent much of his life in the military. He moved quickly and looked none too happy. He ignored the attendees trying to get his attention as he muscled his way to his target, which happened to be me.

"Look at the time," he barked, pointing to his expensive Rolex. "You need to get these people in their seats! We didn't spend all this money for them to take long breaks feeding their faces." I was young and, having been newly promoted, I wanted to impress him, so without further ado, I just began to shout at the attendees. "Show's starting!" I yelped, extending my arms and moving them up and down as if I might take flight at any moment.

I realize now how utterly stupid I must have looked, and I received my share of dirty glances, but darn it if my VP wanted me to get these people to their seats that was what I was going to do. I shooed people away from the coffee, I interrupted conversations, I started to close the doors to the ballroom (in their faces, I'm not proud to say), I had the facility turn the lights on and off, and I had production make the voice of God announcement that the show was starting.

Out of breath and red in the face (mostly due to embarrassment), I stood in the back of the room, astonished I was able to seat 250 people in less than ten minutes. Then, from the front of the room, I was able to make out my VP heading my way.

"He's coming to tell me good job," I thought to myself, preparing for a little praise. Acting like a lunatic was about to pay off and I could not have been happier.

Soon he stood before me, my ears eager to hear his words, I leaned in closer so as not to miss a single syllable. "I need a cup of hot, black coffee with two Splenda before I speak," he stated.

"I'll be backstage." Then he turned on his heel, leaving me to the task.

My perception was that I was moving up. I received a title, a raise, and I was working to make my bosses proud. My boss on the other hand could have given two cents about my title or my raise. To him it was irrelevant. I was still there to fetch coffee and keep his boring meeting on time, so he had enough stage time to get his perceived important point across.

Here is another true story about leadership and limited knowledge.

We had a client event that was being held at a TPC (Tournament Players Club) golf course in Scottsdale, Arizona. The evening before the golf game, we had a nice welcome reception followed by leisure time. I was headed to my room to get ready for bed around 9:30 pm when my boss called. "C," he began, "I'm looking at the forecast, and it looks like it is supposed to rain tomorrow."

His voice was shaky, and it was easy to tell he was panicking a bit. I was aware of the weather, but because the forecast currently called for 35 percent precipitation, I did not feel the need to cancel golf. And I did have a second plan as a backup that consisted of a poker tournament to be held in one of the resort rooms with food and open bar.

I offered up plan B and asked, "Do you want me to go ahead and move forward with poker, or do you want to take a chance on the weather and keep the golf game?" There was a long pause before he replied, "Neither, I want you to move our golf game to the day after tomorrow and move our meetings to tomorrow."

I was stunned. He said it so casually, so matter of fact. Although my first reaction was to laugh at his joke, I soon realized he was dead serious. I took a deep breath.

"Bill," I began. "You know I'd do anything for you, but this is something I simply cannot do." I went on to explain the very reasons why.

1. We were set to play on one of the world's most prestigious and sought-after courses. It was difficult just to get the tee times we had, as the course was booked solid for months in advance. We would easily be able to cancel our game, but no way on earth were we going to get another time later that week or during our event time for the full group of thirty golfers.

2. The golf game was to begin at 7 am. How were we to effectively communicate this change to our clients? It was 9:30 at night. Was the plan to call all the hotel rooms? Put a note under everyone's door in hopes they would read it? Send smoke signals?

3. Opening a meeting room for the business meeting was the easiest item to accomplish, but seeing as the audio-visual professionals and hotel contacts were at home for the night, it would have also been a huge inconvenience for the staff.

Bill was always a bit jumpy when it came to the success of taking care of our clients, but he was also very reasonable. He and I agreed we would watch the weather, hope for the best, and if the precipitation expectation rose above 35 percent, we would call it first thing in the morning.

In the end, it rained, but it rained in the late afternoon after our golf game concluded. Thank you, weather Gods!

But that isn't the point, is it? The point here is education, Bill had no idea how difficult his request was. Nor was it his job to know, it was mine. But the conversation began as a directive, "I want you to move our golf game to the day after tomorrow and move our meetings to tomorrow."

If I were looked at as a C-suite employee, the request would have been presented as such. "Do you think we could move our golf game to the day after tomorrow and move our meetings to tomorrow?" Thus, recognizing me as the expert not the order taker.

It is so crystal clear, event professionals do such an amazing job of making the impossible happen, that it has become expected of us, "I simply love throwing parties here, they are really no trouble at all."

Forbes magazine puts our profession in the list of top ten most stressful jobs year after year. If you have been doing this job for ten hours, ten days, ten months, or ten years, you have figured out why. The organizational skills, attention to detail, and project management required to do this job are monumental. Unlike other company projects, an event is not one you can easily delay. That date on the calendar is coming, it is coming fast, and if you have not planned everything out, it is not going to be successful.

That friend, is the definition of stress. But I love it, God help me I love it. I love our profession, the amazing things we get to do, the privilege of creating something that will live on in other people's memories for their lifetime. It is my calling, despite how hard it is to obtain the respect the profession deserves.

Through it all, I have learned to become a fighter, to develop a thick skin, and curve my emotion into logic. At the heart of it, I really do believe we can gain the respect we deserve, but we must do it together. So I have given this a lot of thought, and I am ready to share the three key factors about why event professionals are locked out of the C-suite.

Get it? Key reasons? Locked out of the C-suite? Ok, enough of that, let us start with number one.

Chapter 3: The first key reason event professionals are locked out of the C-suite

Put simply, everyone thinks they can do our job.

When you tell someone what you do for a living, how many times do you hear, "Oh, dream job!" Or, "My daughter, niece, neighbor, I would be so good at that."? The reason everyone thinks they can do our job is simply that they have no clue what our job is.

It is a common misconception our job is a never-ending party with celebrities and champagne. We have made some strides of awareness in this area, but we still have a way to go before leaders truly understand how our profession contributes to the company's culture, goals, return on investment (ROI), and bottom line.

This is a big reason why there is so much interference during the planning process and why stakeholders tend to select speakers, create content, and construct the timing of the program based on their personal likes rather than follow the guidelines of the multiple studies on adult learning and successful meetings. Have you ever worked with an executive on a speech they were to give and tried to explain to them the adult attention span studies to encourage them to either limit their time on stage or to format their time into increments, giving the audience concrete transitions that will keep their attention?

Odds are they handled your suggestion one of three ways. One, they looked at you blankly telling you to keep the time the way it is. Two, gave you the explanation that their presentation is so important it will certainly defy the laws of the human attention span. Three, they asked you to add even more time to their presentation than they had before. I doubt very seriously they stopped, listened to what you had to say, and then made proper adjustments based on your knowledge of audience engagement.

This type of executive interference can even be more frustrating in our new world of virtual events. As a savvy professional planner, you have done your research on virtual and hybrid events. You may have taken a few classes or even went so far as to become certified in virtual planning. Whatever the learning outlet, the point is you have equipped yourself with C-suite knowledge over best practices and possess the ability to navigate leadership through the planning and execution of a successful online conference. Now whether you can put this education to good use, is another matter.

To illustrate how disastrously things can turn out when someone with no experience steps into an event role, let me tell you a great story about what happened to a dear friend of mine.

Leslie texted me one day with some amazing news. A major A-list, well-to-do movie producer offered her a dream gig to be their personal event planner. The job consisted of her performing all the event duties necessary, including basic planning, the hiring of vendors, theme and décor decisions as well as entertainment selection for all their personal events.

These consisted of everything from A-list celebrity backyard BBQs to family weddings to lush dinner parties, all with very healthy budgets.

I was so excited for her, and we agreed to have lunch to talk more about the opportunity. The producer was well known for throwing massive events and many were covered on social media and celebrity gossip rags. Leslie and I fantasied about all the connections she would make and the interesting people she was sure to meet. Completely caught up in the majesty of it all, I paused to ask her, "So what happened to the last planner?"

Leslie set down her tea. "Um, what?" she asked becoming serious.

"How come the position was vacant?" I asked curiously. The events were well-known affairs, so obviously someone was planning for him before Leslie was hired.

She confessed she never paused to consider why this established and highly influential individual was in the market for a new event professional to meet their needs.

I dismissed the question, not wanting to upset the tone of the lunch or diminish her excitement, "I'm sure they retired of something."

It was not long before Leslie had her first assignment to organize your average Saturday afternoon casual BBQ with "just a few" friends. You know, the kind you typically host in your own back yard with a major rock band performing, unlimited staffed food stations, wine pouring contortionists, and a multitude of bars.

Six months before the event and Leslie was already hard to connect with. She worked tirelessly to organize everything perfectly for her new boss. Knowing how stressful planning time can be, I made a note on my calendar to call her the day after to check-in and get all the details on the affair. But the moment she said hello, I could tell she had been crying. I did my best to calm my friend and, of course, asked what was wrong. What she told me next truly shocked me.

Leslie was on property the day before the party overseeing the final details and assisting vendors with final arrangements like location set up, access to power, decorations, furniture set, etc. The backyard was in the midst of organized chaos. The sound of power tools, generators, and general construction filled the air.

She had been onsite since five o'clock in the morning and as the crew entered the late afternoon hours, she was beginning to see some real progress. The dance floor and stage were intact, the food stations well on their way, and the bars were being stocked when the producer rang her phone to inform her that they were twenty minutes from the house and wanted to meet upon arrival to discuss the event. Leslie, despite having many projects to compete, of course, agreed to the meeting.

Twenty minutes later, she sat on an uncomfortable designer chair she was told was valued at over $10,000. She did not ask for this information, but it was volunteered to her as soon as the producer joined her in the salon (fancy name for sitting room).

The producer approached a bar cart, poured themselves a scotch, added a few ice cubes to the crystal glass, and took the seat before Leslie. "So," they began. "Show me the drawing of the layout."

Leslie reached into her tote bag and pulled out the floor plan to share. She began with guest entry and explained the full experience, pointing out where the stage, executive restrooms, bars, and food service would be. The producer sipped at the drink with their facial expression turning as if they had just eaten a lemon wedge.

"No," they said looking at the design. The producer then went on to aggressively question her every decision and insisting there was no rhyme or reason to the way she had laid out the event. Although taken aback by the abrasive tone of her employer, Leslie joined the producer to point out items on the blueprint that they may not be familiar with.

"These are powerlines." She began identifying the large line with the tip of her pencil. "I know that," the producer insisted. Grabbing the pencil from Leslie's hand, the producer placed the floor plan onto the surface of the coffee table and proceeded to draw their own layout over the one she had worked six months to create.

"The band needs to be here," they said drawing a massive rectangular shape across the yard from where it was planned and subsequently being built.

"Why do you have the main bar here?" they demanded. Leslie began to answer so the lines wouldn't interfere with the dance floor but wasn't given that opportunity before the producer drew a solid circle in another area of the map.

"It should be here," they huffed. This went on for some time, and Leslie's mind raced. What was being asked was nearly impossible, the build was 85 percent complete. She tried desperately to reason with her boss but was cut off each time.

"Do it like this, or I will find someone who can," was the statement that ended the conversation. The producer stood handing her back the floor plan. "This!" they said hitting the paper with the end of the pencil.

"This is what I want, it's what I've always wanted," they claimed. "Now that you have my vision, I don't see how you can screw it up."

Now I know what you are thinking. "I would have walked out of the door." "I would have told them what they could do with that paper!" "I would have quit on the spot and told them to do it them self."

But I implore you to consider what Leslie thought was at stake. This is a highly influential person with numerous connections. The benefit of making this person happy at the time significantly outweighed the overtime she would need to put in to make their vision happen. So, she rolled up her sleeves, paid a ton of overtime, and completed the new floor plan a little after 1 am, the day of the event.

Leslie did not get any sleep despite her exhaustion. She lay helplessly in the morning hours staring at the clock ticking away as her mind teased her with visions of the events to unfold. She imagined food station lines competing with bar lines and confusion consuming the guests as to which line they were actually in. She witnessed collisions on the dance floor when the bar lines crossed paths and watched as stylish ladies in high heels did their best to navigate a field of laid powerlines and prayed over and over no one would fall or injure themselves that day. Unfortunately for Leslie, the continuous nightmare she experienced the night prior was exactly what came to transpire the following day.

The afternoon was bedlam. Guests grew increasingly angry throughout the day, openly sharing their frustration with the order of things. People at the bar area could not hear their conversations because the sitting area was positioned too close to the band. Attendees in line for a drink had to share space with the guests on the dancefloor and more than one was bumped by a wayward dancer. And more than one starlet sprained an ankle passing over hidden in plain sight powerline.

Leslie was in full panic mode and her primary focus was not crying when the producer found her placing small orange cones around the pesky power lines. "You don't know what you are doing!" the producer yelled loud enough for the majority of guests to overhear.

Not having the grace to wait until they were in private, the producer continued the lecture in front of the prestigious guests. "I should have known better than to take a chance on a nobody!" she was told. Leslie continued to endure an extremely unprofessional and embarrassing dressing down that was pointed in the wrong direction.

No doubt this person is amazing at producing films. You have most likely even seen one or two of their titles yourself. Even Leslie will admit the films are good. But what this person clearly is not, is an event professional. It was obvious that they were accustomed to being the boss, the primary decision-maker, and in total control. That worked well for them in their profession, but not so much in ours. A perfect example of someone who thinks they can do our job.

The whole affair ended with the producer not only firing Leslie but also refusing to pay her. They cited the amount they contributed to the overtime needed to set up the event more than covered her salary, and had she done her job, that overtime would not have been necessary. Leslie investigated suing and hired a lawyer, but when faced with a long legal battle and expensive lawyer fees, she ultimately walked away.

When Leslie told me the story, I wondered if this person was being prepped for surgery, would they have the audacity to tell the surgeon how to perform the procedure? Would they demand a local, so they could oversee the work with the use of a hand mirror telling the doctor what to do? If they were headed into a courtroom, would they represent themselves rather than hiring the services of a lawyer? If their car broke down, would they take it to the mechanic only to stand behind them and tell them how to fix it? I could go on and on, but the chances are that, no, they would not. So why then was it so easy for them to question her? Essentially our profession? Why is that so easy?

On the opposite end, when you work to earn the respect you deserve as an event professional, you will find a completely different circumstance than the one illustrated above. Your boss's demands and desires may not always be the best course of action, but when you claim your seat at the table, you can also have conversations like the one I had with a former CEO.

He and I were in the same minivan taking us to a farewell dinner for our top performer incentive trip in Las Cabos, Mexico. As we traveled along the winding road, Skip leaned forward. "Hey, Christina," he began. "I was wondering, what criteria do you use when making the decision on where we will hold our incentive trips?"

Thrilled to get this question and the opportunity to discuss it with him, I went on about how safety, cleanness, language, travel time, weather, overall cost, civil unrest, and currency all went into the decision-making process.

Skip listened carefully to what I had to say and followed up with, "I was wondering why we never went to Hawaii?"

I confessed that not only do I really like Hawaii and no doubt it would be a huge incentive, it was just not a destination with a decent return on company investment. He seemed intrigued, so I continued.

We are a company on the east coast, so getting our attendees to Hawaii would more than likely take a few connections. That's not necessarily a deal-breaker, but when you factor in the time change, you're facing some pretty exhausted travelers upon arrival. Our event was only three nights in length, so it seems like a lot of travel for such a short period of time. I also explained the month we hold our trip is right smack dab in the middle of Hawaii's rainy season, and because we preferred to hold events outdoors, the weather alone was a primary reason to avoid the destination.

I then went on to note Hawaii is among the most expensive locations in the United States and our cost for food and lodging would take up most of the budget. "Just because we have the money, doesn't mean we should spend it," I joked. "I also don't think it would be a very good look for you to show the board that the cost of rewarding our top performers is more than the revenue they brought in."

He chuckled, nodded his head, and leaned back in deep contemplation. I wasn't really sure what he thought of my explanation as we continued to drive in silence. I hoped he was pleased. I ran over the conversation in my head thinking that if I were CEO, I'd want my non-revenue staff to put a good amount of thought into these decisions.

Skip remained quiet through the drive. As our van pulled up to our destination, I remained in my seat waiting for him to depart. When he stood, he patted my shoulder and said, "That's why you're in charge."

I could have floated into the dinner. To obtain a seat at the big table, to gain trust, and be the decision-maker, you need to prove you are being a good steward of the company and its goals. Being able to answer questions like this without hesitation and with solid reasoning was critical in this instance.

I have to say, I could have discussed this topic all night, but Skip got what he needed and gave me the sense that he was proud of me. This is a memory I truly cherish.

But enough of memory lane. The first key reason event professionals are locked out of the C-suite is because everyone thinks they can do our job. Couple that with the perception our job is just a Champaign guggling position of non-stop parties, and we are beginning to have a bit of a problem on our hands. These two factors also directly contribute to the second key reason event planners are locked out of the C-suite, so let's talk more about that now.

Chapter 4: The second key reason event professionals are locked out of the C-suite

———————————

Our profession is not defined.

If you are in the job market or ever have been, you have more than likely encountered this issue - searching for jobs with events in the title only to stumble across some rather interesting postings whose definition of an event professional is creative, to say the least.

Below is an example of a job description someone actually sent me after reading my profile online.

Event Specialist

We are looking for a creative event professional to increase sales, get buyer's attention, and provide an excellent in-store event experience.

Responsibilities

- Define, design, and implement a creative visual merchandising strategy
- Create appealing and eye-catching events that lead the customer through the entire store
- Identify key messages and set a clear image of the end result

- Come up with, revise and present design ideas with assistant merchandisers
- Act in alignment with the organization's culture, products, image, and target market
- Monitor costs and work within the event budget
- Oversee the production and brief staff on arranging displays
- Change displays to promote new product launches and reflect festive or seasonal themes
- Liaise with suppliers and source elements

Clearly, this is a product display job, so why is it titled Event Specialist? Is our skill set that confusing to hiring managers?

This is a big problem, especially when you are looking for another job. I have come to the conclusion our profession is so undefined and misunderstood companies really do not know what they want when it comes to event staff. They think they have an idea of what they need, but when you get into the role, it is obvious they did a quick copy and paste from another site that had a similar job opening.

Case in point, I was looking for a new job. Of course I applied for roles matching my previous title (director of events) and that is the title of the job for which I interviewed and subsequently landed. This was the type of company that invests a lot of time and effort to find the perfect candidate. You know the ones that have their candidates complete skills tests, timed ethical quizzes, and personality tests before having you sit physically for an interview.

The interview process was intense, and it gave me the impression they knew exactly what they wanted. But two weeks into the role, I sat at my desk popping aspirin like candy reviewing the latest "event" my team and I had been tasked with - to organize the company's holiday party at a nearby BBQ establishment.

I would have laughed out loud if I wasn't so confused. I skimmed the requirement sheet I had been given: find a willing employee who will fit into the Santa's elf costume, arrange a secret Santa exchange taking into consideration employees' families and guests, organize a find-the-pickle contest, and set up holiday karaoke.

Frankly, I was stunned. I went from throwing conferences for more than 3,000 people, hiring Grammy award-winning acts, and working with A-list celebrities, to walking around a corporate office with a mason jar full of employee names for a secret gift exchange.

I reached for my job description; maybe I missed something? Nope, no matter how hard I looked there was nothing about finding the right size person to fit in an elf costume.

I remember it started to rain, and my mood turned somber to match the weather. I thought to myself, what in the hell were they thinking? Yes, them. I did nothing more than apply for a role that completely matched my experience and skill, and they could have easily accomplished this event with a staff volunteer. I was way over-qualified felt mislead.

I talked myself into believing this was just a blip, something they wanted me to do before it was time to start planning the big stuff discussed in the interview. I went to have a chat with my boss about the upcoming calendar of events and when maybe my talents would be best utilized. I told him I would have the holiday party wrapped up by the end of the week, but if he could go ahead and give me some insight into the next project, I could start working on that as well.

He eagerly informed me after the holiday party, my team and I had the office Mardi Gras celebration to plan. When I asked him about the large events, he told me those took place every three years, so I wouldn't need to bother worrying about that for a long time.

I looked at my bank account and decided I could depart this role after the Mardi Gras celebration and got my resume back in order. How sad to have spent only a short while there and had they known what they needed, my time and theirs would not have been wasted.

To provide more context on what the director of events was expected to do, the Mardi Gras celebration was held in a conference room at the corporate headquarters. I attended no less than eight in person meetings to discuss important specifics like where the king cakes should be ordered from, what beers and wines should be ordered (they owned the building, so alcohol could be served), where the food should be ordered from, and what the décor should look like.

I was overwhelmed and unprepared for the amount of time and effort the whole staff seemed to spend on these decisions. I thought my eyes were going to stick to the back of my head as many times as I rolled them! I received no less than three visits a day from co-workers sharing their ideas for the two-hour gathering. All day, I entertained suggestions like, "I was thinking, you should order real-live crawfish and boil them in the parking lot, because you know crawfish are only good if they boil on the spot." Or "Don't buy the cheap little beads, no one likes those, get the big beads, the ones with stuff on them like shrimp or street signs."

I listened to all the requests, gave my report on the progress at staff meetings, and did as I was told. I ordered plastic masks and beads from the well-known drivel-making website that shipped the order. I splurged on green, purple, and gold linen tablecloths and ordered the king cakes from the authentic New Orleans bakery as instructed. I was able to procure New Orleans beer and wine and also brought in a frozen hurricane machine. All the while, I slashed out days on a calendar until my departure, like a recently convicted prisoner.

On the day of the event, I had about 20 unsolicited employees come "help" me with the set up. They tore into the boxes, set up the bar (all the while enjoying some libations), put up the highboys, and ordered about the catering team when the food showed up. It was maddening. If you are like me, you have a plan of where things go, even for a silly company gathering, and here I had people just taking that plan and tossing it straight out the window despite my protest.

I remember one woman in the office, who I suspect went for the director role and didn't get it, was unnecessarily bossy this day. She found me in the chaos to let me know the king cakes had arrived. I walked with her, showing the table I dressed for the cakes. I had used pans and cake plates to create some height to the table and then draped the surface in a gold tablecloth so each cake would be at a different level on top of a gold backdrop, which I thought made for a nice display for the eight cakes.

She looked at it and then asked me where the place cards were that showed the flavor of each cake. I looked at her blankly because this was the first I'd heard of it. With a haughty tone and her hand on her hip, she said, "We ALWAYS have place cards, so people know what flavor they are eating."

Thinking this to be one of the more ridiculous conversations I have had in my lifetime, I controlled my urge to shout at her and simply replied by telling her I would go make them straight away. In the solitude of my office, I checked the time. In five hours this would all be behind me.

I quickly printed the cake cards and returned to the bedlam that had become the conference room. I approached the king cake table to see my co-worker had completely rearranged the table, so that all the cakes were sprawled on a flat surface. If that was not bad enough, she also had removed them from their boxes. This meant it was now impossible to identify one cake flavor from the other since they were all decorated the same.

I stood there, holding useless place cards and asked her as calmly as I could, "Which one of these is the raspberry cream?" She looked at the table and then the trash bin. After realizing what she just did, she replied, "They all taste the same anyway." And then walked off.

I shook my head. No joke, my title was director of events, and here I stood before a flat, boring pastry display holding identification cards for cakes that, unless tasted, could not be identified. It was a truly mind-boggling experience. In this person's eyes, my display was wrong, because it was not something she would have done. But she did not have the forethought to complete the project correctly.

It was at that moment that I decided to let go, and I mean let it all go. After all, this was my last "event" and pretty much my last day. So, with nothing left to give, I hit the hurricanes. I hugged up on that little frozen machine, filling my cup one after the other, and observed the party from a distance.

I watched my co-workers gorge themselves on gumbo, crawfish etouffee, and jambalaya. I witnessed them rip into the king cakes, dropping frosty crumbs about the room and trampling them into the bristly, grey carpeting. The already noisy room reached fever pitch. Each time someone nearly choked on a tiny plastic baby, I would toast each victory by refilling my plastic cup with a fresh hurricane.

When the event ended, I sat in an empty room with an empty hurricane machine and an empty feeling. I let this visual sink in before reaching for a black plastic trash bag to start the cleanup. Gone were the 20 eager employees who just had to assist with setup. Missing in action was the snippy colleague who flattened my unidentifiable cake display. Nowhere to be found where any of the company's leadership or even my own boss. No, just me, dirty dishes, empty beer bottles, smooshed carpet cake crumbs, and my beloved hurricane machine. Which, it turns out, was the only helpful item in the room that day.

How was it that the same exact position and title, director of events, was so vastly different? I chalked it up as a fluke; certainly I was the only one with this issue.

Well, that was my first thought until Leslie, fresh off the movie producer fiasco, found herself in this situation. Again, on the job hunt, she sat down and searched for event professionals and found a nice director position perfectly matching her skills. Of course she applied.

The interview process for this company was fairly uncomplicated. Leslie put in a résumé, conducted a phone interview with HR, advanced to a phone interview with her hiring manager, secured the face-to-face interview with the hiring manager, and aced the final interview with the CEO before receiving an offer. Everything appeared to be on the up-and-up.

Then exactly one week into her employment, she found herself sitting in a conference room with a staff member who proceeded to enlighten her on her "real" job. The young man explained to her that her job really just boiled down to waiting on the leadership team hand and foot.

"You will need to fulfill the desires of the upper management staff," he informed her. "You will need to be especially attentive to our CEO's wife."

Leslie was a bit taken back, to say the least. This was the first she heard of catering to management in this way and was especially surprised by the mention of taking care of someone not employed with the organization.

She was skeptical, after all this was her employee, yet he spoke to her as if he had the authority to dictate her job responsibilities. She encouraged him to continue. He gleefully proceeded to tell her she would be spending her time making restaurant reservations and creating custom menus, which did not necessarily match the standard restaurant menus.

Leslie was confused. Sensing this, the young man interjected, "You have to be sure they are served broccolini with every meal, whether it's on the restaurant menu or not."

Leslie's head was spinning.

"Also, you will need to make a reservation for yourself at the same restaurant where they are having dinner. You won't be able to sit with them, but you will need a table there just in case they run into any issues during dinner."

"Isn't that what the servers are for?" she asked.

"No, they will want you there to address it with staff."

He continued with her list of duties, which also included hosting hospitality suites for the VIPs during conferences. "You will want to equip the suite with food and beverage suitable to the leadership team."

He pointed out who liked red wines, white wines, what the preferred vodka was, and diet restrictions.

"I'll get you a good list to start from," he assured her. "You can get most of what they like from Publix."

"Publix?" Leslie questioned. "Can't I just order this from the hotel?"

He laughed. "We don't have a budget for that. No, you will need to shop for these items before the event. I suggest you use an empty suitcase to transport the materials from your car to the suite, but don't use valet unless it's complimentary per the contract."

Leslie's brain struggled to comprehend this conversation. This was the first she was hearing about restaurant reservations, babysitting dinners, broccolini, or hospitality suite stocking. At no part of the interview process was ANY of this mentioned to her. Also, the attitude her employee took when explaining was off-putting, to say the least.

"We have six people on the team. Certainly, we can all share in these responsibilities," she reasoned. He looked at her blankly then shook his head.

"No," he said quite forcefully. "We were told that when you started, we never had to do this work ever again."

Although Leslie didn't see any red flags during the interview process, this was a big one waving right in her face.

"It has to be a joke," she assured me. "I can't have this bad of luck. What are the odds of working for that nightmare producer to now accepting a job as a professional executive babysitter?"

I suggested she give it a go, maybe this guy was overreacting and perhaps it was not as bad as he portrayed. I had never heard of a director of events sitting alone in a restaurant on standby to handle problems while grown adults enjoyed a meal. What could possibly happen that a group of 20 grown C-suite-level adults couldn't handle? Boy, were we wrong.

Leslie lasted a couple of years in this role and experienced some amazingly horrific behavior. The young professional who sat her down to explain her duties actually downplayed the expectations the VIPs had of her. Throughout her tenure Leslie endured all of the following:

- It was the night prior to the start of a rather large conference. Leslie was in San Francisco attending a dinner with a couple of co-workers when her phone rang. The VIP of Sales frantically explained to her that she had left her cell phone in her taxi and demanded that Leslie drop what she was doing and call her carrier to expedite a replacement phone for the following morning.

Despite Leslie having to obtain all the information and detail that the VIP of Sales could have easily explained to her own cell phone provider, Leslie was expected to comply and have a new phone sent the following day.

- On a separate event, the room the executive team selected for dinner was too small to accommodate all those in attendance. To mitigate the problem, Leslie put herself and her staff in a small room adjacent to the larger meal room. Mid event, the head of marketing burst into the room yelling at the top of his lungs admonishing her publicly accusing her of behaving as if her team were special.

- Numerous negotiations were held with restaurant kitchen staff about broccolini. Leslie spent countless hours explaining the proper temperature, the sauces expected to be present, and in more than several occasions begging them to add the side dish to their menu.

- During a tradeshow conference the kitchen experienced a mild fire that delayed the delivery of morning breakfast for booth staff. Before Leslie could explain this, the head of IT lost his mind when he arrived and found out there was no coffee. He proceeded to accuse Leslie of treating the executive team as second-class citizens and was quick to let her know that if he didn't have his coffee within the next ten minutes, then she could take the next flight home to pack up her desk.

- When traveling abroad, Leslie was sure to travel in a day early so that she could scope out the nearest convenience store. She would arrive, quickly unpack her personal items, and then carry her empty suitcase to the store to stock up on wine, liquor, snacks, and serving utensils to place in the executive's hotel rooms before they arrived. She would tell me of her embarrassment being in another country putting everything into her luggage while trying to muster though the language and currency barrier.

So many more examples could be shared, and yes, her role was defined as director of events.

Leslie and I did a comparison. I left my job as director of events, where my staff and I conducted high-end conferences, education meetings, customer events, and incentive trips, to become the director of office holiday parties. Leslie departed her role as director of events to work for an out-of-control egomaniac only to find herself as director of restaurant reservations and hospitality suites. Either we had some serious karma debt to pay off or our industry has an identity issue. We agreed with the latter.

If businesses do not know how to hire for their needs, how are we to search and find the right role that will enable us to best use our knowledge and skills to assist the company from the start? It should be well known it is not ok to strap a title to a job description and say, "Yeah, that looks about right." If we cannot match our capabilities to their desires, then we are in a lose-lose situation. In both cases, the companies could have hired a much less skilled professional and paid them half the salary.

To that point, I have also seen this in the reverse, where the title coordinator or specialist is applied to a rather lengthy and robust event job description best suited for a more seasoned event professional like a manager or even director. That is just as lousy as overpaying a professional for a coordinator role.

Companies are clearly confused. While they seem to know the skillset they want, they do not know how to correctly advertise for it or set the pay scale to the level of professionalism they need. Overpaying for a skillset is bad business and underpaying is shady. Frankly, we deserve better.

We represent a multibillion-dollar industry. I would wager it is much larger than the one you are working for. Never mind any small decision made on an event will impact the outcome in some way, or that you are educated in how to make cost, time, and quality decisions that impact the event or contribute to how the attendees feel about the product and company. Forget all of that, because until our profession is defined and companies fork up the correct pay for our experience, it will always be hard to land the right role at the right pay. We are at the mercy of the hiring companies to know not only the skills required for their role but also the proper compensation for these skills.

In a later chapter, we will discuss the interview process. I will share some tips on how to dig up red flags during the proceedings, so you can make an informed decision on whether that particular role is right for you. For now, let's stay on topic and dive into the third and final key reason we are locked out of the C-suite.

Chapter 5: The third key reason event professionals are locked out of the C-suite

Us.

The sad truth is, despite how many people are in our profession or how many titles exist, there are very few professional planners who can do the job at the level the profession requires and deserves; and that, my friends, is a major reason we are held back.

This drawback is so critical that I will harp about it for the remainder of this book, and I have labeled it "the curse of the unschooled planner."

You know 'em, you work with 'em, and you may be in a position where you must deal with 'em. These are the quintessential "that looks like a fun job" planners. Little to no training, they have no desire to educate themselves. They do not attend classes. They do not read books. They just like the idea of traveling to places and putting on a party, and because ours is not yet a profession that garners its due respect, they get employed.

These are the planners who did a really great job with their sister's birthday bash and nailed their best friend's bachelor party and, while I don't wish to generalize, they most likely pronounce the "l" in salmon. Most of them tend to sing instead of talk and usually add an "a" at the end of their sentences, i.e., "That's grroosss-a."

Ask them how many bartenders are needed for a 100-person reception, and you will more than likely get a blank stare and a response like, "I dunno, enough so that everyone gets served," followed by a giggle.

Have you had to deal with this yet? If not, consider yourself extremely lucky!

There is truly a massive danger with unschooled planners in that they represent us and our profession. They contribute to the idea we have a fun job that doesn't require a lot of skills and, therefore, we need to be told exactly what the stakeholder wants. It's also why stakeholders feel it is okay to toss changes into the program up until the day of the event.

The more we continue to employ and put up with planners who do not know what they are doing, the more we will only be viewed as the fun department that parties for a living. The exact image we must combat.

Here is a tale of two planners; one professional, one unschooled, and how they were asked to work together. Hint: this does not go well.

Due to a recent merger between two companies, two separate teams are working together to plan an executive leadership meeting for 350 people in Arizona in July. So already you're thinking, that's hot and not a "so pretty" hot but rather temperature hot. The three-day event required a welcome reception, breakouts, general session, meals, and farewell dinner.

Some context here, both teams had been working independently for their respective company for a series of years enjoying the planning and execution of events that fell in line with their individual company's culture and budget. Team A, worked for the larger of the two corporations and had a healthier budget, larger staff, and were educated with many of them holding their CMP or in the process of obtaining it.

Team B worked for the smaller of the two corporations, had a smaller staff, smaller budget, and no one on the B team had or was working toward their CMP. When the companies merged, the CEO of the A-team was dismissed from their post and the B team's CEO was appointed to lead the newly merged company.

It is important to point out that team B director of events was close dear friends with the newly appointed CEO. It wasn't long after the merger that these two teams moved to shared office space and were told to work together to achieve company goals until leadership was prepared to make a decision about which of the directors would take full reigns of the team moving forward.

As you may have already guessed, the tension is high, the air ominous. Rumors and hearsay quickly spread, both team's favorite topics of conversation became the perceived shortcomings and attitude to the other team. A member of Team A would walk into the restroom and two members of B would stop talking, cough a little, and pretend to be washing their hands or checking makeup. Members of Team B would pass the working space of Team A members and they too would stop talking and change the subject quickly. To avoid confusion moving forward, I will refer to the director of the A-team as Thomas and the director of the B-team as Kathy.

Well, Thomas and Kathy of course become quick enemies, each striving to outperform the other, or as Kathy would do, withhold information from Thomas in an attempt to control the upcoming events and take full credit for success.

This would be the case of the Arizona leadership meeting. Although Thomas and Kathy were both tasked with the planning, Kathy quickly took control by omitting Thomas from pre-planning meetings with leadership and not sharing with him or any members of his team the decisions made or provide any follow-up on changes made with them. Kathy planned key meetings when Thomas was out of the office, stating it was the only time leadership was available, but she also managed to keep members of Team A off the guest list, as well.

As the date of the event approached, Thomas began to ask questions regarding the event, and he was more than surprised to discover all most every aspect of the event had been planned already. He barely knew the hotel name much less any other important logistics.

Two weeks before the event, Kathy scheduled the in-office pre-con with leadership and was begrudgingly compelled to invite Thomas. She reasoned that although the invite must include him, it would no doubt show how inclusive she was being.

Thomas showed up to the meeting ready to learn the plan for the event for the first time. Kathy opened the meeting by waving her hands in the air and painting a picturesque image of the perfect Arizona location that of course contained perfect weather and oh-so-happy attendees. "It's simply going to be divine," she exclaimed before moving through the logistics of the agenda.

Kathy is singing words and adding "a's" to the end of her sentences when she comes to the location of lunch. "Lunch will be outside on a terrace-a," she announces quite happily. Thomas takes a hard look at the notes and notices that despite the terrace being uncovered, there is no weather back-up listed in the information provided.

As Kathy continues the meeting, Thomas begins to investigate and flips through the floor plans. He is a little more than surprised to see the terrace Kathy selected is 100 percent exposed to the elements, no roof, no conditioning. "Arizona in July," he thinks to himself.

Pulling up the weather forecast Thomas discovers that the expected temperature during the day will be 104 degrees Fahrenheit with clear skies. Realizing this problem, he searches through his packet looking for the weather backup but failed to see where one was listed.

"I'm sorry to interrupt," Thomas began. "But, can we go back to lunch for a second?"

Kathy looks as if she just ate a lemon but controls her emotion enough to smile and sputter, between gritted teeth, she said, "No problem."

"What did you have a question about?" she asked as nicely as she could.

"I'm looking at the weather, and I'm concerned it will be uncomfortable for attendees. I'm looking for weather backup, and I can't seem to find one."

Kathy blinks twice. "So?" she asks.

"So, what is the plan if it's too hot to eat outside?"

Kathy begins to hope that the deodorant works as the label promised. "What do you mean?" she says, stalling for time until her brain can think of a proper comeback.

"I mean what I asked," Thomas replies. "What is the backup plan if it is too hot to eat lunch on the terrace? I looked up the weather forecast and it's showing temperatures in the 100's with clear skies. Since the terrace is completely exposed, I'm wondering where our attendees can comfortably eat lunch if necessary."

Thomas can hear a few executives at the table shifting through their packets to confirm. Kathy has narrowed her stare as if willing Thomas to keel over in his seat.

"The hotel is booked, so there is no backup plan," she confirmed, but then quickly added, "But, it's a dry heat, which is very lovely and my onsite contacts say we shouldn't anticipate any problem."

She continues the meeting by changing the subject, and since no one questioned her further, the issue was dropped.

Thomas was admittedly dumbfounded. He knew something had to be done, so he made a quick note to revisit as Kathy began to discuss the plans for the farewell party. This event was planned to take place poolside, yet another outdoor location without a weather backup.

When the meeting concluded, Thomas returned to his office and ordered a climate-controlled tent to cover the terrace. He was frankly surprised by these decisions and began to wonder why the hotel had been selected in the first place. He would never book a location that couldn't offer weather backups.

Curious and considering that maybe they got a heck of a deal, Thomas pulled up the contract to investigate the cause of the decision. Looked like a typical contract, no big savings, the opposite really, the resort appeared to be on the expensive end. But then he found something in plain black and white that might have directly contributed to the decision. Kathy was to personally receive a healthy amount of hotel points for the contract. He shook his head not really knowing what he could do, if anything, with that information.

Admittedly, the tent was a bit more expensive than he wanted, so he called a meeting with Kathy and their boss Melony to review the purchase and the reason behind the decision. Thomas felt strongly he needed to take attendee comfort into consideration and that, because so many decisions were made without his team, it was about high time someone demonstrated some good judgment. When Thomas explained this decision, Kathy was visibly livid.

"You have no right to make these decisions!"

Thomas defended his position and Melony, a tall mousy woman who typically ended most disagreements by siding with Kathy, shocked Thomas by agreeing to keep the tent.

"Ok, but just how are we supposed to make room for this in the budget?" she sneered, thinking she got the best of Thomas with that question.

"I'm glad you asked," Thomas admitted, pulling out the budget spreadsheet he received in the meeting the day prior. "If we scale back the attendee gifting, we can easily afford the tent."

He pointed out that the gift order included items like handmade leather messenger bags at $350 apiece, company-branded $200 visa gift cards, and three pairs of designer socks at $30 per attendee. Thomas discovered long before this meeting that to compensate for lack of industry knowledge, Kathy and her team showered attendees with gifts to woo them.

Kathy reacted as expected as if Thomas had just suggested she eat dog poop. Her face flushed red as she argued leadership deserved to be showered with gifts and it was expected.

Melony listened to both sides and although she didn't ask to cancel any of the giftings, she did include the tent. Thomas felt relieved, but he certainly didn't feel like he had won.

Make sure your seat is in its original, upright, and locked position and your tray tables are stowed as we prepare for our landing in Arizona.

Thomas knew he was left out on some necessary meetings but just how left out became more evident during the security tour. As the team was led by security to the ballroom, the production crew was loading in equipment, and Thomas noticed hundreds of white leather office chairs on wheels. The crew was in the process of placing these chairs along the stage in the general session room when Thomas stopped a member of the team to ask "What are these chairs for?"

"These are the chairs the audience will be sitting in," he was informed.

Thomas took note of the room. It was a three-tiered room and octagon in shape. The ground floor would serve as the main stage and was surrounded by three tiers, each about three-feet high. The tiers did not have any railing or protective barrier between them, and the chairs on wheels were being placed on these leveled tiers. Thomas rolled his eyes at the sight.

"Whose genius plan was this?" the head of security asked. Thomas of course knew but wasn't in the habit of tossing co-workers under the bus, so he didn't answer. One thing was clear, he and Kathy were significantly at odds on how events should be conducted, and leadership had no clue how at risk they actually were.

As far as the tent was concerned, it was a hit. The week of the event, Arizona would experience record highs and with the terrace positioned in direct sunlight, it would have made for an extremely uncomfortable lunch. The addition of the tent proved to be crucial and not just for lunch. As luck would have it, the evening farewell event, originally planned to take place poolside, was rained out. Not just rain, but a massive thunderstorm.

Kathy reluctantly, and with no real choice in the matter, had to make the decision to move the event to Thomas's tent. You can only imagine how this made each of them feel. Kathy was frustrated and bitter for being so wrong, and he was elated and justified for being so right.

Thomas enjoyed the evening, grinning and happy to have been able to provide the solution. Kathy overindulged at the bar, removed and sullen, only managing to smile when a member of leadership approached. If Thomas held his breath waiting for her to thank him for making the call to add the tent, he would have passed out from lack of oxygen.

Insult to injury, on the final day of the event, as leadership was closing out the general session, the CEO asked Kathy to the stage to congratulate her on a job well done. Thomas knew immediately neither she nor Melony informed leadership of his contribution to the success of the event. He also knew this put him at a significant disadvantage about who should take leadership of the event department. He worried if he took it upon himself to go leadership and explain what happened, he would risk looking like a bragging, non-team player. Although Thomas was not prepared to admit defeat then, it became crystal clear Kathy would ultimately be promoted over him even when post-event results showed the event was over budget by $2 million. Kathy would not be held accountable for a cent of it.

As expected Kathy was promoted to Senior Director. The unprofessional planner who didn't have weather backup, placed attendees in danger by putting them in wheeled chairs on a raised platform with no protective railings, ran over budget, and received a hefty pile of hotel points. I challenge you to tell me of another profession where this would have happened.

This story is one of many examples of where leadership is so unconcerned with the event profession that they really have no idea what level of damage an unschooled planner can actually do. Kathy was able to fib her way out of being held accountable for the overage in budget and outwardly blamed hidden production costs, shipping costs, and taxes. Hidden or just not factored in?

What every CEO should know is unschooled planners cost them money. Just as in the example above, an unschooled and unprofessional planner can cost them in ways other than just the obvious of going over budget. Kathy put her attendees in jeopardy by placing them in an unsafe environment and she did so willingly. She opened her company to lawsuits. Think about if any one of her attendees had wheeled themselves off a platform, injuring themselves or others. Or say the tent had not been there and someone experienced heat stroke. Her decisions and general lack of planning ought to have been reprimanded, but instead, she was rewarded with promotion, given the keys to the event kingdom to continue to overspend, make poor decisions, and put the company at risk.

Unschooled planners are a liability to companies financially and to professional planners in reputation and job importance.

Daniele is as unschooled as they come. She was sent to Las Vegas on a final site inspection for a program that was three short months away. Upon arrival, she was picked up in the hotel's limousine and delivered to the hotel lobby, where her hotel staff and contacts eagerly awaited her arrival. After shaking hands, Daniele announces she is hungry and demands they take her to lunch. They comply.

As it was explained to me, she sends her first plate back with an overly disgusted face and "pouts" until her second plate arrives. After lunch, the hoteliers (again busy with other things) suggest they walk the space and begin the final planning. Daniele, on the other hand, has alternative plans. She announces that because she just got off a long flight she will need to rest a bit before they can review anything. She goes to her room, orders room service, and three hours later sends a text to her contact letting her know she is now ready.

The hotel contact is staying late to accommodate Daniele, taking time away from her own friends and family. Daniele makes minor but bitterly sarcastic and rude comments like how she does not approve of the carpet design and how it is dirty in spots. Then she holds her nose as she walks through the kitchen area.

Fast forward to a week before the event. Daniele realizes that she will need more VIP transfers and hotel suites than the number outlined in the contract. It also looks like she is going over budget on food and beverage and will require some help in getting creative. However, due to Daniele's unprofessional and rude behavior during the final site visit, her contact is reluctant to assist in providing any more than is in the contract.

I had an opportunity to sit down with the hotel contact who told me this story. When I asked her for an estimate of additional fees Daniele cost the company, just by being rude, I was told it was around $25,000.

Right then it was evident to me we have a real problem in our industry where this type of behavior goes largely unnoticed by leadership. What is the real cost of her behavior? It's easy to add up the $25,000 but what about the cost extending beyond this dollar amount? Like the relationship between client and vendor? It is unlikely any future requests for proposal from Daniele's company will be taken seriously. Even after she has moved on, how long will it be before the trust returns? The lack of motivation to work with these personalities potentially has long-lasting effects.

I know of many vendors that have simply passed on Request for Proposals (RFP) based on a company's reputation. If vendors are in a spot where they can overlook occasional clients, they will certainly do so to avoid dealing with unschooled professionals. In many cases, the choice to pass on a proposal wasn't as the result of their own experience but that of their industry contacts. Yes, word of mouth is still the most effective form of advertising.

Here's a story to illustrate just how damaging a company's reputation can be. Company Inc. had a long-standing relationship with a local hotel we will call Uptown Resort. Company Inc. held the same large conference year over year for the past ten years at

Uptown Resort. They occupied the same space, same dates, and the same number of hotel rooms, which were plentiful. Each year the staff of Uptown Resort dreaded the entire process of planning and execution with Company Inc. They found the staff to be rude, uncompromising, unprofessional, and, of course, unschooled.

Company Inc.'s leadership was no better, if not worse. Demanding, unyielding, and boisterous. Uptown Resort's staff found they had to work extra hard when Company Inc. was in-house because they were often misinformed on event orders, audiovisual needs, and event timing. Every year without fail, Company Inc.'s CEO would dress down a resort staff member publicly for a situation that was ultimately due miscommunication by Company Inc.

So in year ten, toward the end of the conference one of the planners from Company Inc. realizes they do not have a contract signed with Uptown Resorts for their conference next year. Easy enough mistake to make when dealing with long-term, multi-year contracts. But here is the kicker: when they brought this to the attention of the resort, with full intent to sign another multi-year contract, the resort let the planner know they had already sold the desired dates and space to another company for years to come. This partner of ten years sold the space without giving Company Inc. the first right of refusal! Seems pretty obvious to me the hotel was happy to get rid of this client, their unrealistic demands, and entitled attitude.

Hilariously, the CEO of Company, Inc. was so angry he announced, red-faced and quite loudly at an employee meeting, that he would NEVER use Uptown Resort or ANY hotel in their umbrella because they "sold our space." This was not an uncommon threat he made to almost every hotel chain you can name.

I imagined the staff of Uptown Resort popping champagne and dancing about as Company Inc. scrambled to find a new home for the following year. Why? Leadership is one thing and it can be difficult, but the relationship between the company and vendor is the responsibility of the planner. Professional planners can navigate rough waters when leadership is difficult, mitigating a polite and mutually beneficial relationship.

An unschooled planner at the helm will typically facilitate a poor relationship between vendor and leadership. They will often blame the vendor for their mistakes and poor decisions causing leadership to hold the wrong party accountable. The bottom line is unschooled planners directly impact our reputation, partnerships, and industry.

We have a responsibility to the unschooled planner as well as ourselves. If you can identify one on your team, please mentor them if they truly wish to make event planning their career. Lift them up to professional planner status. Now on the other side of the coin, we also have a responsibility to direct them out the door if they cannot cut it.

Chapter 6: On your mark, get set...

Before we go on, allow me the opportunity to give a small pep talk as to why this journey you are about to embark on is so important for not only your but our entire industry.

We are making progress towards being taken seriously. We are consistently told of our importance; how, when people meet, they can change the world. We have education programs, accreditations, and even universities coming out with bachelor's and master's degrees in event planning. We have numerous publications and our friends at Meeting Professionals International (MPI), the American Planning Association (APA), the Events Industry Council (EIC), and many others truly doing their best to get the word out. Their efforts should be applauded, but the truth of the matter is they can only do so much.

Yes, the information is there and the data exists. We can tell each other all day we are important, making ourselves feel all warm and fuzzy; but, guys, this information is not making its way to the C-suite. I do not know of any CEO who is going to research what it takes to be a Certified Meeting Professional (CMP) on his or her time off. The importance of the event planning team does not make it to the agenda for board of director meetings, and audits are not being performed about the effectiveness of these teams.

I had an interview with a company that was entertaining the idea of bringing events and meetings in-house and starting a department. They brought me in to discuss this. I am here to tell you it was a great, dare I say, perfect conversation. I came prepared with charts, graphs, articles, and examples of my work. I showed how, through tough negotiation and savvy spending, I could pay for my own salary. I spoke about how an in-house, dedicated meeting and event resource will add value and help create a company culture; how a planner on the inside included benefits like knowing where every penny is spent; and how a salaried employee would have a vested interest in the company's success, thus promoting trust in the in-house planner.

The CEO's executive assistant was present during the conversation and chimed in to say she had neither the time nor skills for creating events and really did not like doing it. How about that? An executive assistant admitting event planning is not a skill set of her role? HUGE!

The meeting lasted about three hours, with them telling me I opened their eyes. They went on to say our conversation was one of the better business meetings they'd had all year.

Two months later, I received a call from the hiring manager, who said she was sorry but the company could not afford the luxury of an event planner at that time. I was stunned.

"I'm a luxury?" I thought. I mean, I agree, but what?!

Why are human resources (HR) departments so trusted? Why does leadership listen to what HR reps have to say without question? Sure the HR team protects the company from lawsuits, but so do we! Of course, HR does other things as well, benefits, insurance, employee mitigation, but there is a reason they are listened to without question. The *Harvard Business Review* published an article by Dave Ulrich titled 'A new mandate for Human Resources.' In it, he talks of the importance of partnership with key leadership and why HR is so important. Since its release in 1998, it has been used by many HR professionals to argue their place and guess what? It is working.

Meeting professionals deserve this level of trust as well if, given the opportunity, we can save the company not only money but time and quality. When we explain adults don't learn by listening to a talking head, through boring PowerPoint presentations, or speeches exceeding fifteen minutes (because after that everything is in one ear and out the other), people should listen without question.

I have often wanted to tell leadership to just take the money they are spending on the event and flush it down the toilet because that is essentially what they are doing if they do not want to follow the guidelines to keep the audience engaged. I cannot tell you how many times I have sat in the back of a packed room watching as one-by-one attendees checkout, start playing on their cell phones, and begin to talk among themselves. All the while ignoring some pretty important information from the mainstage.

Hey leadership, ever wonder why you can't fill the first two rows of a session? It's the fear your attendees have they will actually have to pay attention or pretend to pay attention throughout the entire session. Ever notice how you don't have that problem during an award or entertainment program? Because, they know those sessions are going to be entertaining and fun.

If you have a problem filling your first few rows, then you most likely have a reputation for conducting a boring session. It's just too much stress for your attendees to pretend to care. They prefer instead to sit middle to back and blend into the crowd, so they can mess around when they inevitably and understandably reach their boredom threshold. Flush the money, or better yet, just give it to your event staff. I promise they will take it.

We all know our worth and what we can bring to our company and profession. So, it occurred to me - it is up to us. We must start a grassroots campaign from the inside. We must be our own voice. We owe it to ourselves and those coming up. This is now an inside job that has to start with us. We must speak up and often within our own organizations and to those that contract us.

I have held several positions where my team and I were trusted and viewed as a viable department greatly contributing greatly to the goals and value statements of the company. In these cases, my team and I worked in tandem to create stellar events, always able to show our value. We were direct and honest with ROI, even suggesting the cancellation of some events that did not reach the goals set by leadership. We were ethical and treated company money like our own. In return, we each had the ear of the CEO and his immediate staff. But make no mistake, although I technically had a seat at the table, each and every day seemed to bring on its own struggle to stress the importance of our role.

Almost every event team can relate to long days and late nights of planning, double-checking, evaluating, and working on fictitious simulations to better the process. If I personally had a dollar for every frustrated, tear-filled situation, I'd wager

I would have had enough money to buy Miami. It's not easy to work to achieve company goals while simultaneously working to achieve the status of a valued, trusted, and viable department worthy of making decisions on behalf of the company without constant leadership input.

On the teams where I felt most valued, I more often than not held trust and a seat at the table, sometimes years before being given a title and salary to compensate my contribution. I fear this is where we are stuck as a profession. I'm sure many of you reading this book hold a similar position but can't seem to scrape past a senior manager or director title. Is it not frustrating to hold an important role only to be constantly overlooked for promotion?

I've become a bit of an authority on obtaining a seat at the table because I once had to endure having eleven bosses during fifteen years. Think of that, eleven bosses in fifteen years. Each one of them with different ideas, thoughts, and opinions on how our company events should be run. Anywhere from entertainment choices to vendors to venue selection - let me tell you, they were all over the place.

I had to "sell" myself, my team, and our talent for every new boss. That alone proved to be a full-time job. It was a complete and utter restart with each new boss, and believe me when I tell you, I heard it all from each of these individuals. Some got it and let us continue to be successful; and others didn't, fighting us along the way, seemingly challenging us, and refusing to listen to reason. Just because they thought it was their duty to do so. Strange how some leaders do that.

But anyway, for most of these years I worked under the title of a senior manager. Two upsides of having a new boss nearly every single year is I perfected a step-by-step approach to being seen as a valued employee worthy of a seat at the table, and I've learned to manage numerous personalities and management styles. These are two critical skills for navigating one's way to the role of respected trusted and valued employee.

I recall it was around 2015 when the pendulum began to really swing from a buyer to seller's market (a trend that lasted probably all the way to the pandemic). I was well aware of the shift, having had many conversations with industry experts and reading several articles. I knew it wouldn't be long before meeting room space would be challenging to find, and food, beverage, and hotel rooms' costs would be on the rise.

I worked with my industry friends and compiled an eight-page document supporting the reasons we needed to consider multi-year contracts with venues. The document illustrated past and future trends and outlined how much these types of contracts would ultimately save the company in costs as well as peace of mind knowing that we had secured space for the future.

I presented the document to my then-boss Dolores, sliding it across her desk, asking her to please share the findings with leadership at the next meeting. She didn't even read the first page. Instead, she placed her short, stubby finger on the documents as if she were touching a dirty piece of garbage and slid it back toward me saying, "They won't go for this."

I tried again, placing my well-manicured, slender finger (bitter, party of one) on the report and sliding it back to her.

"Then you need to help them understand the potential implications if they don't go for it," I explained.

Delores once again slid the document in my direction.

"They won't listen."

She smiled. She actually smiled!

I made one more attempt.

"Then make them listen," I implored. "Isn't that your job as the leader of our team?"

She lost a bit of her smile, but not her malice.

"The answer is no."

I left the office, completely dejected. She didn't even read the title page. I was so passionate about the content, however, I covertly arranged for a lunch with the company's CFO the coming week to discuss the findings of my research. I figured if Delores wasn't going to listen, I was going to find someone who would.

My lunch date proved a success. Our CFO took the document, reviewed it, and brought it before the executive team. Despite Delores's attempt to stop me, I was bold enough to circumvent her block and took the information to the top. Why? Because I had an obligation to that company to arm them with the proper information to make educated decisions.

I was given permission to sign contracts up to eight years in advance, and Delores lasted a few more months before being ushered to a new role. This was a pinnacle and a bold move, one that could have easily backfired had it not been for the steps outlined in this book.

Look, trust and autonomy do not come easily. If it is a professional goal of yours, then you must prepare for the fight. The good news is, I am here to help you when it gets hard or you just don't think you can do it. It's not an easy road, but it is manageable. I think you have been told by now that life is not fair. I'm sure you have. I think this especially rings true if you are an event professional. Not only do we have to work hard to prove we are worthy of a seat at the table, we also have our job to do.

To put it simply, this is not a profession for the delicate. That being said, I just love it. It's my calling and my passion. I will wager that if you can identify with the stories in this book, you have had similar experiences. And if you are still in the profession, then you totally understand where I am coming from. You care about this industry and your job gives you pride. I hope you also agree that it's up to us to fight to raise awareness within our own organizations. We don't just order danish and coffee, we don't need to put up with being second-class employees, and we certainly don't care if you're too cold. Yeah, you heard me.

Chapter 7: Why we do not care if you are cold

A dear friend and I signed up for a public speaking workshop out-of-state. It was a seven-day program that focused on projection, mannerisms, and content. On the final day of the class, we were to be videoed as we performed a how-to presentation on a topic we knew a lot about and enjoyed. I naturally selected how to plan an event.

On the third day of class, we were instructed to have an outline of the points we needed to cover to effectively convey our topic. That evening, Lee and I met in his hotel room with a bottle of wine to compare notes. He happily shared his outline, an outstanding job, as usual.

Then it was my turn. I retrieved my notebook and began to deliver the content of my outline.

Determine the goal of the meeting

Work with stakeholders on meeting specifics

    Space

    Attendees expected

    Meals offered

    Breakouts/workshops

    Trade show space needed

    Branding / theme / engage marketing

Source a location (may need to visit several)

Contract for the desired date

>Add concessions

>Add desired clauses

>Check for indemnification

>Outline exact space and room block needed

>Review with a fine toothcomb before signing

Request for Proposal for the appropriate vendors to match your goal and budget

>Equipment (staging, sound, internet, power, man-hours)

>Food and beverage (budget consensus)

Entertainment (expectations, airfare, transportation, hotel room, cost, management fees, expectations)

Transportation (equipment needed, VIP transfers)

Re-visit venue with production staff

Work on layout

Food stations and bar areas

Staging

Seating

Obtain fire marshal approval

Meet with stakeholders, agenda, production needs, and timing for speeches

Re-visit venue with stakeholders to review layout, promote trust

Communications – invitations, dress code, set clear expectations

Create website/app, including agenda, dress code,

Security and risk assessment

Weather

Disasters

Emergency needs for attendees

Review budget/goal / check-in with vendors for room pickup

Put agenda together

Which breakouts go where?

General session speakers

Secure speakers and entertainment

Share with stakeholders

Engage destination management company for any off-site dinners/celebrations

Find a location for the event and follow venue steps to contract

Select food for each day

How much coffee / where breaks need to be

Remember backstage / production crew / load-in and out

Re-communicate with attendees

Social media blast

Marketing materials

Focus on agenda

Adjust to changes coming in

Determine set up for breakouts based on adult learning and goals

Classroom / theater / rounds

In-room beverage service or community break in common areas

Timing of breaks and timing of breakouts

Communicate to breakout trainers and speakers

Share layout and timing

Seek approvals and ask for needs (materials, whiteboard? Projectors?)

Stay engaged with the vendor

Signage and wayfinding – directional staff? Volunteers?

Staging design / seek approval

Common area branding

Revisit site with vendors and stakeholders (if needed)

Sew up transportation

Send in manifest

Ensure correct contact information is obtained

Review rooming list against registrations

Note VIPs for hotel

Have pre-conference meeting with hotel staff

Have pre-conference meeting with transportation

Ensure all attendee communications are correct to agenda and expectations

Where to pick up the bus?

Schedule for transportation times

Who to contact if they have concerns?

Work with the security team on evaluation and emergency plan

Who is to be contacted for shortness of breath/injury?

What happens if the lights go out? Etc.

Adjust agenda and ensure they are copied on all media so everything is correct.

Complete rehearsal schedule

> Make sure speakers know to rehearse
>
> Entertainment rehearsal

Complete needs for any gifting

> Shipping
>
> Receiving equipment

Set up planner office and war room

> Power/internet for all rooms

Ensure equipment needs are met for breakouts

Uniforms for volunteers and staff......

Lee patiently let me get this far before taking a sip of wine and reminding me the speech was only supposed to be ten minutes in length. I stared at him blankly before throwing the notepad across the room yelling, "How in the hell am I supposed to do that?!"

I realize this contradicts one of the key reasons we are omitted from the C-suite. Even though I hate to admit it, the truth is that at some level everyone is an event planner. There, I said it.

People have had at least some small part in planning weddings, birthday parties, anniversary parties, and, sadly, funerals. This contributes to the belief that everyone thinks they can do our job.

Some people, like me, are addicted to stress. I get a rush when a problem comes across my desk before the event. I also celebrate the wins when something goes wrong onsite, and the team works together to overcome it. I'm here to tell you, while I've probably not been through it all, I've been through some pretty substantial situations like power outage, internet down, fire alarms going off, sprinkler systems going off during outdoor events, political protests, public transportation strikes that shut down trains, taxis and buses, candid camera crews attempting to sneak into the general session, earthquakes, snowstorms, hotel worker strikes, heart attacks, fistfights, and most recently a pandemic. There is a solution to every problem, and you must be the type of person who is not going to run when the shit goes down.

The amount of responsibility we have on our plate is tremendous. The outline is a great illustration of this, but it is truly just the tip of the iceberg. The list goes on and on and each of these points even has its own micro bullets and so on. The amount of detail behind each danish, coffee break, projector, power supply, hotel room booking, correct badge spelling, location of meeting room, and wayfinding signage is astonishing.

The truth is attendees come out of breakouts and general sessions without any thought as to how the speaker got hired. Little contemplation is given as to how the whiteboard they used in the team project was there along with colored markers. They think not of the effort it took to provide the diet soda and cookie they grabbed at the break, or that everything they see, touch, feel, taste, and hear was made possible by their event professional. The fact they have a place to stay, transportation to the venue, credentials with their name on them, gift bags, and a chair to sit on are all made possible by the event planning team. They enjoy the event, the entertainment, and the experience with no consideration to those that made it all possible.

But this is truly our lot in life. To perform the near-impossible and be the one everyone goes to when something lousy happens. When there is a cancelation needed, you are asked to negotiate that, when the lights go out in the ballroom, all eyes land on you, it can be anything from an earthquake to a fire alarm but one thing is for certain, everybody in that room is going to turn to you no matter the size, no matter the role, stakeholders, hired speakers, your bosses, production staff, and attendees are all going to look at you with a mixture to confused, angry and imploring faces that all scream one question "What do we do now?" So why the inability to view us as professionals? Why, when I complete forms online and when I get to the dropdown for occupation, is event planning not present? Why will a company promote someone who doesn't know what CMP or CMM is, over someone who has dedicated themselves to their profession and company?

It's time we shake things up and bring attention to our true worth. More than ever the microscope of how we contribute to our company is directly upon us and we now have a unique opportunity to not only change things in our industry but also illustrate our professionalism to our leaders. We have had to pivot from live in person events to offering exciting dynamic and well-attended virtual platforms. If you were a planner during this time who waited for your leadership to tell you how to conduct a virtual event, you may need to consider picking up an industry publication, attend an online course, or seek new employment. Our profession is constantly changing, and we need to grow with it. I cannot stress enough that it is time to make a difference and that difference is not only defined by us but is navigated by us as well.

So to the nitty-gritty and the reason you picked up this book, in the following chapters I will give you the step-by-step formula to pick the C-suite lock and take your rightful seat at the table. But know this going in, this journey is not for the faint of heart, it will require some hard work and is sure to take you out of your comfort zone. Being held in the highest regard and trusted to perform your job with minimal supervision is not given lightly. If you desire to have this and other perks like the authority to sign contracts without leadership review, staff, or freedom over your work calendar and office hours, then you have to start with a single realization, this is going to be hard work. I can give you a formula that will help you obtain your career goals, but I cannot guarantee you a fancy title or corner office to accompany your seat at the table. I can only guarantee that if you commit yourself to these steps, you will have the respect and autonomy you seek. No, this is not going to be an easy journey, but if I know one thing about you, you are an event professional and that alone qualifies you for the journey, so let's go.

Chapter 8: The first step on your journey to the C-suite

The first step to obtaining your seat at the table is education. Yours and those you work for. Through education, you will arm yourself with the ability to perform at a higher level and, in turn, educate leadership about your role, worth, and profession. It all starts with a very important component - education.

Now, if you already hold your Certified Meeting Professional (CMP) or other accreditation, kudos to you and a huge pat on the back. If you don't have it, it would be in your best interest to go get it. The CMP designation is quickly becoming the pinnacle event professional certification you can possess. I've seen more and more job descriptions that prefer or even require applicants to have it to apply. I'd wager they don't really understand all it takes to earn it, but it is being requested. That alone is a big step in the right direction.

Now a little disclosure here. A CMP is not going to make you a professional planner, just like a bachelor's degree does not mean you are a scholar. Degrees are truly wonderful things to have, and they prove that you have committed yourself to learning. Higher education will enhance your resume making you more attractive to potential employer's but having a CMP will give you a huge competitive advantage in this industry.

Now, I know many stellar event professionals who do not have their CMP, but they have experience and knowledge that surpasses the need to obtain the designation. It is merely that companies are beginning to recognize on some level they should be looking to employ a professional, which is highly encouraging.

If you are employed and kicking ass as a non-CMP event professional, I still encourage you to go for it. Not only is it a great program, but it's a great refresher on current industry trends. If you are planning on going for it, please refer to my list of resources on the final pages for a stellar study program I highly recommend.

Now, whether you have your CMP or not, you will want to subscribe to at least five meeting publications and dedicate a day each month to digesting them. Yes, you have that right, digest them. It is not enough to simply read them, but you must also study them. As you do ask yourself the following questions:

1. On a scale of 1-10, how relevant is this knowledge to me?

If you have answered this question with a rating of 6 or higher, move on to question number two.

2. Is this content I can use right now or will this be useful later?

If you answered this will be more useful later, then develop a system to file away for future use and set-up a time in the upcoming months to revisit it. I use Outlook for this. I put a meeting on my calendar to remind myself to review my future folder and have found this works well. If you answered this is useful right now, then move on to question number 3.

3. Should I share this content with my team, my boss, or my leadership?

If you answered yes, then create a plan to share the here and now. Email is a great tool to forward this content, but if you overuse this technique, your emails will fly into the trash bin faster than empty Red Bull cans after a 3 pm break. So be sure to take your time and craft a message that includes how you think the content is relevant to the business.

There are plenty of publications out there, and I realize that most of them cover the same topics, but repetition works. The point is to start and build a quiver of information you might be able to use during the next meeting with your boss or, even better, should you find yourself in a conversation with your boss's boss. A list of publications I recommend is available in resources at the end of this book.

You should also attend industry conferences and online courses. If you hold your CMP, you must acquire continuing education to recertify, but there is no law written that you cannot exceed the required hours. Some of my dearest friends and valued industry contacts have come from attending industry events, both physical and virtual. Open yourself to learning and partner with someone who can and will hold you accountable for the training. When I took a class on becoming certified in virtual events, I asked Lee to join me so we could hold one another accountable. Often these types of classes are much more fun to take with a buddy anyway.

If you are part of a team at work, you already have a group of people who can not only make education a goal but also hold one another accountable. It is a good idea to appoint a team member as the education steward. This staff member should be tasked with acting as support for all education needs of the team. Duties may include:

- Identifying CMP classes, study groups, online resources, and ordering study material for members who are in pursuit of the designation.

- Track education opportunities for the entire team. Search for online learning, review industry events to assess relevance.

- Responsible for writing a business case to support teams' participation in attending conferences and industry meetings for leadership support.

- Track the team's education units, ensuring memberships are up to date and keeping a calendar for re-certifications.

- Assigning publication articles to team members for sharing at the next department meeting. This is especially great to help staff with public speaking skills and presentation organization.

- Facilitate open discussions on industry trends, breakthroughs, and new technologies like hybrid event planning, virtual engagement, and market forecasts.

If you appoint an education steward and follow education guidelines, you will find you and your team will be armed with quick facts and knowledge that can easily be worked into almost any conversation with any member of leadership. It must be understood education is the first and greatest weapon in the fight for professional freedom.

I realize that obtaining a CMP is not cheap or accomplished overnight. If you are lucky enough to work for an organization that supports your personal growth, then you will want to have a conversation with your leadership on starting the process of becoming a CMP. If you will be paying for this out of pocket, I suggest speaking with a tax professional to see if you can claim the expense for the tax year. If you're not sure if your company will pay for it or not, it's worth looking into. When I asked for company support, I created a business plan that outlined my commitment, and also the benefits the company could expect from my education.

When I obtained my CMP, I didn't just print out the certificate and hang it in the office. No, I perfected an elevator speech I could easily recite, letting all those above me know what it means to be a CMP. I composed an email highlighting what the achievement meant and sent it to every VP and above in the company. It was nice to receive the obligatory congratulations from everyone, but that would not be the last they heard of it. I insisted they understood the accomplishment. I mentioned my studies at the water cooler, the breakroom, and, yes, even the bathroom. Any opportunity that presented itself to discuss what I learned, I took.

Over time I began to see results. I started to receive more questions from leadership about my ideas for company announcements and product launches, and I was asked to join more meetings. I knew beyond a shadow of a doubt my efforts were paying off when the senior VP (the one who demanded a cup of coffee from me during the leadership meeting in San Francisco) asked for my thoughts in a staff meeting.

You heard that right. He stopped the conversation to ask my opinion. You could have knocked me over with a feather. Despite being a little intimidated, I managed to intelligently answer his question without hesitation or lack of confidence, and I'm quite proud to say he never asked me for coffee again.

Education is a critical first step, but it is important to point out you are playing the long game. You must be strategic in your approach in sharing your knowledge. Resist the urge to invade the next leadership meeting and dump a boatload of stats and knowledge on the team all at once. It will not only fall on deaf ears, but you run the risk of appearing desperate.

If done correctly, you will gradually start to see a shift in how your leadership approaches you. They will begin to ask for your opinion on changes rather than just demanding you make them. You start to receive better communications. For example, instead of someone demanding, "What is the cost of the projector we are using in general session?" you will be asked a much more kind and thought out, "When you have the time, can you send me the cost of the projector we are using in the general session room?" Leadership will start to view you as a productive team member who is focused on many logistics and treat you accordingly.

Now, when you acknowledge this shift, be careful not to claim a premature victory. It is going to take time and, remember, you are playing the long game. You must continue to keep up with and invest in your education. Once you begin to recognize the shift, it's time to start asking for additional funding for you and your team to attend industry events in person or virtually to obtain more knowledge as well as develop more industry connections.

I recognize it is hard to ask for money to support the education of a non-revenue producing department. Recessions, pandemics, and company health can contribute to being told funds are not available for this. And face it, no one likes to be told "no".

So here is where bravery comes in. you must be brave enough to ask for any resources you need to support your role. When suggesting to leadership that you or your staff attend industry events, I highly recommend doing some homework. Present a business plan outlining the key reasons for attending. Include the benefit of face-to-face meetings and, in addition to outlining the topics you and the staff will learn, illustrate how you will apply this knowledge upon your return.

Do not oversell it. Part of getting the company to support your future education is making good on your promises. If you tell them, you will learn a certain skill and bring it to the business, you will need to prove it or risk losing credibility that will prevent future support. Remember to think strategically and put yourself in leadership's shoes, if you were in their position, what would you need from your employee to consider the proposal? Then do that.

Yes, it's really that simple. You may be told "no", but that's ok. Look for the next opportunity and continue to ask in a professional and composed manner. Ever hear the "squeaky wheel gets the grease"? Well in most instances, this is correct.

Even when you get that seat and obtain your goal, commit yourself to continued learning. Set a time on your calendar about every six months to re-identify your weak and strong areas and continue to structure education based on your assessment. Locate courses, lectures, books, and articles on those topics.

I was having a hard time with contracts, from a general understanding to wanting to be sure I included items important to me. I took a course that was being offered during an industry conference and was so impressed with the presenter, I asked if he would be willing to train my staff.

Once we obtained the knowledge, we presented contracts to our leadership differently. We pre-highlighted information we knew they would be most interested in, like force majeure and indemnification, but then drew attention to the clauses we added like aesthetics and a detailed cancellation agreement. We also focused on the additional concessions we included and were able to give an additional dollar amount we saved by including these.

The repetition of this method resulted in leadership telling us they no longer needed to see the contracts and that we had the authority to sign all contracts on behalf of the company. I did send them a quarterly report on what we signed, how much we saved, and where we were going for the next event.

Another example of how my education made my career easier was in the form of pre-event communications. I was frustrated by the whole process because I took a lot of time and energy creating a comprehensive and informative pre-event communication only to seemingly have it ignored by my attendees. It was evident as the event drew near my message was not getting through. I received questions previously answered in the pre-event communication, so I took another look at it.

Granted it was a lot of information, but I did use bullet points and even called out the FAQs as a quick reference. Still, it didn't seem the majority of attendees grasped the information. It was infuriating, and I was getting increasingly upset. No one likes to repeat themselves.

Then, through my studies on adult learning, I found the majority of adults capture and retain information when it is first presented in short, sweet burst like bullet points, and then is followed up with some sort of visual representation.

Knowing this, I was able to re-vamp my communication style. I created and sent the usual detail but began to follow up with photos and captions to communicate important topics like dress code, start times, etc. Experiencing success with that, eventually, I transitioned to a pre-event video featuring characters and skits to communicate important event details. Guess what? It worked!

A personal career highlight occurred at a casual cocktail hour. Contradictory to cocktail receptions in the past, this one we allowed jeans to be worn and stressed that in prior communications. Of course, you already know one attendee showed up in khakis and felt compelled to complain. I noticed him approaching me, already knowing by the look on this face, the topic of his conversation.

"No one told me it was ok to wear jeans," he whined. "I feel like an idiot."

I was about to reply to him when quite out of nowhere a fellow attendee interjected asking him, "How could you have missed it? Not only did they advertise it in the 'things to know before you go," he reached out, taking the badge around the khaki wearing attendee's neck and spun it around to show him the back. "It's also written on the back of your badge."

I could not have been prouder, especially since the attendee who did this was one of the worst offenders of claiming not to know information on site.

It is for these and many other examples, I cannot stress the importance of consistently keeping up with education. It truly is not only a career enhancer, but when used to illustrate your worth, it's a game-changer. There is an abundance of information out there for you to tap into; The American Planning Association (APA) Meeting Professionals International (MPI) Professional Convention Management Association (PCMA) Events Industry Council (EIC) to name a few. All you need to do is dedicate time and effort to investing in the studies and participate in the organizations.

Now, obtaining and having industry knowledge is highly important, but I also need to stress that you really need to also educate yourself about the company you work for. To gain respect and be a C-suite-level employee, you need to walk the walk. It is not easy being a non-revenue generating department, so you must be able to demonstrate that your knowledge is aiding the company in hitting company goals in other, more creative, ways.

Face it, it can feel a little weird to hold an events position within the company. Others have a product or service to sell, and you provide a means for educating staff, rewarding top performers, and setting the stage for client-facing or company education. So, it's important for you to educate yourself on the goals of your organization by being a good company steward.

Learn the company mission and value statements. Pay attention when leadership sends messages regarding a new product or introduces a new plan. Then figure out a way to align your professional goals to complement those of the company.

A great exercise is to dissect the company's mission and value statements and brainstorm how you contribute to each. For instance, say your company as value statements such as work smart, put customers first, share accomplishments, and integrity above all. Take out a sheet of paper for each value and write the statement at the top leaving room for your work. Now evaluate each statement by adding two or three bullet points under each to illustrate how you directly impact them. Example:

Work Smart:

· Audit of existing hotel contracts (added aesthetics and pandemic clause).

· Adjusted room commitment for the 2021 midyear event based on current predictions for business travel. Saved $123,000 by reducing rooms.

· Completed my certificate on conducting successful virtual events.

Customers First

· Designed meeting agenda based on most recent event feedback, keeping customer's desires top of mind (invited favorite speaker back, made room for more breaks).

· Allocated complimentary junior suites to top consumers and company supporters.

· Working on a customer reward program where top consumers receive discounted convention passes or complimentary gala tickets.

Share Accomplishments:

· Working with leadership to create team awards to be given out during the gala program at the annual event.

· Adding budget for two additional home office top performers to be included in sales incentive trip to Mexico.

· Working with an employee of the year to present at the next company meeting on the secret to their success.

Do this exercise until you have two to three bullets for each company value. If your company does not have a set of values, do it for the overall mission statement. Think of what you've done to accomplish those goals. Even if your company's value statements include generating revenue, you can always note the savings you achieve through concessions, pivoting to a virtual rather than physical conference, etc.

It's important to note here educating yourself on the industry and educating yourself on your company are two different disciplines. You need to sew them together to show how your discipline and professionalism help to achieve company goals. The perfect platform to achieve this is by using past event survey results. As a professional planner, you should have access to the survey results from your events. You can therefore track event return on investment (ROI) and determine if the event's success was worth the money spent.

I have had many people ask how you can track event ROI. Many think this is something that can't be done, but I am here to tell you it can. All you need to do is compare survey results to the overall goal of the event. Let's say the goal of the event was for the attendees to network and make new connections. What were the post-event survey results regarding these questions? If the attendees answered favorably when asked if they made new connections or felt the conversations had been of value, then you can attest that the ROI is high for this event. Now, on the other hand, let's say that was the primary goal, but there were no questions on the post-event survey regarding the networking opportunities, well now you have a larger responsibility and that is to revamp your surveys, so they ultimately track event value.

Because you have all the data from the post-event survey, you know better than anyone what worked and what needs improved. You know what attendees want more of and great tidbits of information like who their favorite speakers were. Tie these pearls of wisdom to company values. For instance, when recommending a favorite speaker for the next year, reference that this would be a great way to put our attendees first, as it shows we are listening to them. Coming up with an idea, presenting it, and linking it to a company value is a big win and little by little will help you get that seat at the table.

Later, we will discuss what to specifically do with this information once you have gone through the exercise. But for now, let's recap education.

Education recap

1. Obtain CMP or other industry accreditation.

2. Subscribe to at least five industry publications.

a. Make a plan to read and digest content monthly.

b. Share findings if you deem them worthy of leadership attention.

3. Attend industry online and live courses.

4. Obtain a study buddy.

5. If you work on a team, appoint an education steward to track and develop education plans for the team.

6. Identify your weak areas and focus learning on those disciplines.

7. Review company values and mission statements, coming up with bullet points to illustrate how your job contributes to the organization's goals.

8. Review survey results from previous events for tracing ROI, recreating survey questions, and making suggestions on future improvements.

9. Keep talking, raising awareness, and be slightly annoying to leadership with all you know, how you contribute, and suggestions for improvement.

It may seem like a lot, but remember, this is a journey. These changes will not be overnight, yet a gradual climb to your rightful place.

The second step is not as time demanding, and it's not only a quick process but a fun one at that.

Chapter 9: The second step on your journey to the C-suite

I was the only manager to have a private office in the entire building. Office space was reserved for director titles and above, but due to my standing with leadership, I was granted my own office. That was until Rhonda came into the picture. Rhonda was appointed as my boss for a very short period and the day we met she was settling into her space, the office next to mine, when she came around the corner to peep in my door asking me.

"How come you have an office?" followed by, "You are ONLY a senior manager."

I disliked her right away. I went on to explain to her it was because of the sensitive material I dealt with coupled with the extensive phone conversations I had, which others found distracting on the floor. Since she had absolutely no event background, my immediate goal was to illustrate my team's value in hopes she would want to work and partner with us rather than feel compelled to make changes.

During the seven long months we worked together, I did my best to educate her on the team's accomplishments and how and where we saved the company money and contributed to the bottom line. But all of my efforts seemed to constantly fall on deaf ears. She was immune to understanding a word I said. It was puzzling, to say the least. It's really not rocket science, so either I wasn't doing a good job explaining my role or she wasn't listening.

I was becoming exhausted, and I suppose I inadvertently made my disappointment known. One particular Monday, I returned to work to find Rhonda moving my possessions from my former office to a cubicle just outside her door. She greeted me with an empty box, and I vividly remember her smile as she spoke.

"It's not really fair you are the only manager here with an office, so I went ahead and had you moved to a cubicle like everyone else."

I spent that day moving my items from my old office to my new cubicle. I did so in utter disbelief, and I will admit in embarrassment. Rhonda conducted business as usual, laughing on the phone and holding meetings behind her closed door. I was just waiting for her to ask me for a cup of coffee.

When I had all my belongings moved, I sat for a moment taking it all in. "Did this really just happen?" I thought. A few co-workers came by looking for me and were equally surprised to find me sitting in the cube.

It was mid-afternoon and close to closing time when I finally decided to do something about it. Reaching for the office phone, I quickly dialed Rhonda's boss's extension. Jeff and I had known each other for a long time. I met him early in his career when he was just starting with the company and the two of us developed a quick friendship. He was fast-tracked through the leadership ranks and now, as the Sr. VP of Sales and the boss of my current boss, he was in a place where he could help me.

I talked calmly with Jeff, letting him know there had been a mistake. He listened patiently as I reminded him the reason, I had an office to begin with was due to the private conversations and confidential paperwork I dealt with daily.

"Jeff," I began. "Remember I have some pretty candid conversations over here. I'm negotiating entertainment, incentive programs, and my cubicle is located right beside the customer service department. Think about that, do we really want a customer service representative to overhear the plans to reward sales with an incentive trip to Aruba? Can you imagine how that might make them feel?"

Jeff laughed and stopped me right there. He admitted he was unaware Rhonda moved me and promised he would take care of it at his earliest convenience. He did let me know it would take some time as Rhonda was a new employee of his, and he didn't want to give her the impression he didn't support her.

Jeff did as he promised. He began to slowly support me by educating Rhonda about my role and the important conversations I had. He was hoping she would concede and put me back into the office herself, but she never did make that suggestion. So instead, he moved me himself. The process took about three weeks in total.

It was a Thursday afternoon when a member of facilities arrived at my cubicle to inform me I was moving back into the office. He and I were in the process of moving my belongings and checking the internet connection when Rhonda appeared in the doorway.

"What is going on? "she demanded. I was genuinely surprised she didn't know, so I informed her I was just told to move back to the office.

"How did this happen?" she demanded waving her arms about the room. I found her level of dissatisfaction unsettling, so I suggested she speak with Jeff about it.

The point here is the second step is building an Army. See, Rhonda underestimated my relationships. She didn't consider her new boss knew me on a personal as well as professional level and was a fan of my work. Jeff was a full-fledged member of the Christina Zara Army and because of his personal growth within the company, he was a five star general in that Army with enough clout to support me and power to make changes for my benefit.

Make no mistake, creating an Army is not about sucking up to the higher-ups and doing favors for them so they do favors for you. No, that is not what an Army is about. Building an Army is an organic process that takes time. These are the people in your company who will support and help you because of your professionalism and relationship with them. Just as a regular Army, there are ranks within your personal Army and all people play a big role in your success.

At the heart of it, your Army is your support system. Those within the walls of the company understand your goals, help you achieve them, and point out when you are on the wrong path to victory. They are critical to your success and need to be nurtured, respected, and taken care of regardless of position.

One of the most important members of my Army happened to be the young man who refilled our kitchen and office supplies.

I had little to nothing to gain from him in terms of professional development, but he was someone I looked forward to seeing each day. Through our jokes and stories, he made my day-to-day office life so much more enjoyable.

The story of Rhonda is a great example of what your Army can do for you. She was new and didn't understand the relationships or reputation I had. It's never a great idea to go above your boss, but when you have the right team working for you, it's much easier to do and with less pushback as a result of the action.

Do not recruit by dragging out the company org chart and go after those in high positions. Two reasons this is a bad idea. Number one, it's disingenuous. And number two, org charts can and often change on a dime, so your efforts are most likely in vain. The best way to recruit for your Army is to simply be nice.

Let us be honest, during your career you will have more than your share of reasons to be angry or bitter. After all, you are an event professional. But I beg you to rise above it. We all deal with the sharp, unhelpful emails; being held accountable for things we cannot control; even having to manage jealousy from co-workers who buy into the idea that ours is a sexy job consisting of celebrities and parties. I implore you to rise above it.

As event professionals, we simply do not have the luxury of negativity on the road to the C-suite. The honest truth is, we must work harder, smarter, and with more enthusiasm than our counterparts. People who can keep their cool, remain helpful, calm, and troubleshoot under duress stand out. This trait is not an option for event professionals. We must remain calm and in control no matter the situation. These are the attributes that will not only get you noticed but also attract senior-level members to your Army.

Tara was a master at creating an Army. She always has the most up-to-date laptops and company swag, and if her department needed material to be fast-tracked through another department, she could make it happen. Tara and her team worked for a large company, so just about everything, from getting a pencil to releasing an article was bound in red tape. But because of the size of her team's collective Army, they found avoiding the tape and getting their needs met was much easier and didn't have to deal with a stack of forms or office politics.

Truth be told, all the times I have built Armies, I wasn't really even aware I was doing it until they went to battle for me. I am by nature just a fun, grateful person who really enjoys makings people's lives easier. In turn, I was paid back in ways I did not expect or even know were possible. I have two great examples of how your Army can promote you and save your bacon.

The first begins with me getting the flu during one, particularly cold winter. I was out of work for almost two weeks, and a hotel contact called me to remind me that a contract was due for signing. If I missed the date, we would stand to lose a good portion of the space and concessions. I was out of time and another company was waiting in the wings, praying the contract was not signed.

It was a Saturday afternoon and the contract sat on my desk at work. At the time, I did not have access to the building on weekends, but I knew a few people who did. Barry was a single dad who had his kids that weekend. They were out enjoying the winter weather at a park near the office when he took my call and agreed to meet me at the office to give me access to the building and the important contract due that afternoon. Had I not been friendly to Barry over the years, do you think he would have helped me out on this weekend?

This is what I mean by building an Army. It is important to note I was out of extensions on this contract. Also, it was one of those situations where we negotiated for about two months, and this was the final cut-off. It was truly my fault, and we had to poop or get off the pot. The point is, no man is an island, and no event professional should be either.

The second story takes place in Las Vegas. During our event, the planner's office was the target of a thief. Among other items, the suspect took cameras, video game systems, laptops, and cell phones. The morning of the discovery, my team and I were enjoying breakfast when the executive assistant to the VP of Sales phoned to let me know of the robbery.

If you have held an event in Las Vegas, you already know the distance between the conference center and restaurants can be long, and as I darted to the scene of the crime, Lee was already there with several leadership heads. What he told me was upsetting, to say the least. They were standing about, enjoying morning coffee, and blaming the event planning team for the theft.

Yes, let me say that again. Blaming the event planning team for the theft. Lee was my only line of defense as I made my way to the planner's office. He explained that, before my arrival, the leadership team outwardly questioned the lack of security. They scrambled to discover who had keys to the office and pondered who was last to leave, making accusations that directed blame on us.

Lee spoke on our behalf, diffusing the tension by pointing out the security measures we had put in place. He even asked each of them if they really thought the event planning team members, with whom many had personal relationships, were even capable of committing this crime. By the time I arrived, leadership had become sympathetic to me and worked with me to call the local authorities. I had no idea until years later that Lee went to battle defending my team and was successful in diffusing the situation before my arrival.

Your Army will be a critical component to your success, so you must take care of them at every turn. You have plenty of ammo at your disposal to thank them for their support, and we will get to some of these in a later chapter.

Chapter recap

1. Build your Army by being genuine and kind to everyone.

2. Rise above the chaos, remain calm, helpful, and offer solutions.

3. Nurture your Army.

Chapter 10: The third step on your journey to the C-suite

You have the education and support of co-workers, from the janitor to the senior VP of marketing, but obtaining your seat at the table is still not an easy road. If it was, you would not be reading this book.

We have already established our progression needs to be a grassroots effort and an inside job. So here is where the exercises outlined in chapter eight become relevant. Although you have practiced the elevator pitch and sent a few industry articles to your leadership, now is the time to pound home your worth and that means you are going to have to get somewhat annoying. This is the third step, be borderline annoying.

Is this easy? Um NO! Not for many of us. The hospitality industry tends to attract individuals who enjoy making other people happy. However, putting ourselves and our accomplishments first often does not come easy. The idea here is to toggle between being both humble and ostentatious. This is not an easy task, so I've outlined a few tactful ways to be heard without coming off as incredibly pompous in the process.

1. Use the goal process wisely. Every company I have worked for had its employees go through the rigorous task of creating goals yearly. In turn, the employee evaluation process is greatly weighted by the progress of goal completion. My advice to you is not to view this task as a chore. Instead, consider them an easy way to highlight your responsibilities and gain some brownie points. They are a perfect platform to promote your skills, your growth, and show you are a good company steward. Your goals should cover cost savings through expert contract negotiation, plans for personal development and education, survey satisfaction rating goals, and department growth, if applicable.

2. Be in the right place at the right time. Say you have something you want to run by a specific leader, but you can't seem to get on their calendar or you're afraid of how your boss might perceive the meeting if they aren't present. AKA. Boss block. If you are having a hard time connecting, first prepare a quick statement about what you want to discuss with them.

   For example, let's say you want to bring back a popular speaker because they scored well with attendees on the last event survey. You have been unsuccessful in getting approval but know this one person can make it happen. Prepare your statement and recruit your Army into helping you purposefully, accidentally run into them. Say Bill in accounting sits near the target's office, and he sees they are about to leave for lunch. He might place a call to let you know if you leave now, you can probably catch them in the elevator.

Now that you are in the right place at the right time, it's time to be bold enough to annoy them with your statement. For this example, let's say an announcement was made regarding a new product that is coming down the pipeline and talks about how to train the staff are occurring. Well, now is the perfect time to say something like, "I saw that announcement on product A. Great stuff, I'm sure the sales team is looking forward to that push."

They will assume you are blowing smoke and politely say, "Thank you."

Then you hit them with, "We have the virtual leadership meeting next month, maybe Bill Smith is available to present the team with training. He was rated as our top speaker at our last event, so I know hearing this from him will be beneficial to our team."

ZING. You just planted a seed. Don't expect a ticker-tape parade and a promotion right then. This is a marathon, but you do need to know that even if you don't get a reaction at that moment, you have demonstrated to this executive you are someone who is thinking about the company and what's best to obtain its goals.

3. Keep a quiver of statements. Any time you find yourself in a situation where you are with someone who needs to hear from you, make them hear from you. Don't waste these times with platitudes like goodnight, good morning, weather sure is nice today, I like your shoes, etc.

    Make these little encounters count. Have a few canned items at your disposal at all times. These tidbits may be the latest industry trends, how much you just saved on the last contract signed, or maybe good news like you were able to procure the speaker they wanted. The point is to get noticed as someone who is consistently thinking of new ways to better the organization.

Now let's discuss dealing with boss block. Say you work for someone who already has a spot at the table. And maybe they prefer having you under their command, so they can have a say in fun stuff like selecting wines, choosing entertainment, and or even fashion events to their taste. If you get loud and ask for a little of that spotlight to present to the leadership on your own, well that is going to get controversial real fast. So, my friend, if you are in this type of situation, you are going to have to get bold and loud. I realize this is a sticky situation and going over your boss's head is not easy, but you owe it to your company, your profession, and more importantly yourself to remove the boss block from your path. Here are some diplomatic suggestions for dealing with this situation.

1. Getting noticed by the boss's boss – let's say you come across a tidbit of information you know will be beneficial to the company, but your boss can't quite seem to grasp the importance. Take a deep breath and reach out directly to your boss's boss in an email and copy your boss. State clearly what you have learned recently and provide a summary of how you think it can be beneficial. Speak only in logic, no emotion. Stay away from phrases such as "I feel" or "I hope". Avoid write-in specifics like "this will" and "I know".

At the tail end ask for a meeting between you, your boss, and them to discuss further. Now send and wait for your heart to start beating again. Congratulations, you just dipped your toe into the bold pool. Now, wait to see what type of reply you get.

Most likely it will be your boss super annoyed that you "went above their head." To this, you can argue you didn't, because they were copied on the correspondence. Avoid being treated like a child and instead keep the conversation on an adult level. If the email is ignored by the boss's boss, try again at a later time and continue to stress the reasons you feel so strongly. For example:

"Good day boss's boss, I'm just following up on this information I sent last week. I haven't heard back from you, but I want you to consider my proposal. This new process will enable us to establish whether our attendees understood the content as it was delivered and also track if they are using it as recommended. If you have a moment to spare, I would welcome the opportunity to schedule some time with you to discuss further. I'm sure you will be delighted to discover the minimal cost this will take to implement."

As far as I am concerned, any feedback you receive is a bite on your line. If they ask if you have run this by your boss, you can honestly answer you have and want to include them in the meeting. They may reply, "No, I don't have time to read these articles."

While that feels rude, it's still a reply. You can then respond with something like, "I totally understand, and I wouldn't have sent it if I didn't truly believe this will increase attendee engagement by 20 percent. Implementation costs are minimal, and there is a proven and measurable ROI. I would really appreciate the opportunity to sit down with you to discuss further."

If that is ignored, you probably should move on, but know you planted a seed. Maybe just a mustard seed but a seed nonetheless. Although this is discouraging, it should not be the last time you attempt this.

2. You must be bold enough to ask for a meeting with the boss's boss. If you work for a red tape organization, asking for a face-to-face meeting

with the boss's boss can be intimidating, but what company does not tout an open-door policy? Perhaps it is time to give it a try. If that does not work, or they keep pushing you toward the nightmare boss, do not get discouraged. Know that a face-to-face meeting is not the only opportunity to speak to the higher-ups without your immediate boss present see suggestion number one above.

3. A less intrusive method to fight boss block is to simply report on any items you would normally share with your boss to include your boss's boss. Send weekly, monthly and quarterly reports on your team's progress to anyone you think would benefit from the information. The detail should just be a quick outline of department wins and successes; do not go crazy with content or long-drawn-out explanations. Charts and graphs work great for this. The most you can hope for is three for five seconds of attention span when they open the information, so make it pop.

4. Even if you don't have anything to share, but you are experiencing boss block it's a good idea to develop a professional relationship with your boss's boss. Take the time to craft a reply to a company press release they may have recently provided, or congratulate them on a milestone they may have accomplished.

No matter the message, if it's not in person, ALWAYS copy your boss on the correspondence. Not only is it polite, but it also is protocol and will save you some trouble in the long run. It's important with bosses who block that their ego is fed and they do not feel like you have gone behind their back. Remain transparent and rise above their level of petty leadership. Document conversations to the best of your ability just in case there is a feeble attempt to discipline you for not including them or insubordination. I did mention this is a journey, right? A marathon? A fight? Well, it is.

Now, suppose your boss is consistently standing in your way to gain the ear of those above them. For example, when you try to communicate to their boss, they intervene and tell them they will handle this directly with you and not to worry about it.

You are experiencing boss block plus. This is a schooled egomaniac who is highly threatened by you and will make any attempt they can to diminish your presence before leadership. First and foremost, I'm sorry you are in this position. It's the worst!

It's highly unlikely they will be hit by a bus, struck by lightning, choke on their dinner, get kidnapped in a foreign country, or framed for murder, so you are going to have to either leave the company or deal with them head on. Although they have a home court advantage and the upper hand, all hope is not lost.

Using your Army works VERY well in these situations. Now is time for favors and having your Army speak well of you to those who may be hearing otherwise is a good goal. Everyone's situation is unique, so you will need to assess the best and safest way you can maneuver around a boss block plus.

I am sorry to say, how your boss personally treats you or how they make you feel is irrelevant. Stay clear of complaining about them. The trick is to highlight your accomplishments, not how this person makes you want to scream into a pillow or cry in the bathroom. Mind you, their poor treatment of you must remain within reason. If you are being harassed or bullied, it is a totally different matter.

Dealing with a boss block is no fun. Rely on your Army to carry you through these times, but know complaining outside of your most trusted circle will reflect badly on you. Even though this individual is making decisions that might be preventing growth, affecting the quality of your product, engaging in unethical behavior, or costing the company money, you don't have much of a leg to stand on unless you can prove the negative behavior to leadership and/or in a court of law.

If you have concrete, caught red-handed proof, and it's not just your word versus theirs, document the proof and head down to the HR office. Let's face it, the odds of getting proof will be pretty difficult, so in the meantime, vent with your most trusted Army recruits and document all interactions. I know it is time consuming, but you will be happy you did when you need it most.

Always keep in mind that we as event planners really do make the impossible happen. We magically seem to add hotel rooms, ballrooms, offices, and time on agendas. We do everything in our power to meet the needs of stakeholders and attendees, so asking for a bit of the spotlight and recognition for that hard work shouldn't be considered controversial.

It truly sucks that we have to work just a little harder to get noticed and taken more seriously than our friends in HR, legal, Marketing, etc., but if you didn't like a challenge, you wouldn't be in event planning, to begin with. Show them your worth over and over and then over again.

Chapter recap

1. Use your education to be a squeaky wheel.

2. Get noticed by the higher-ups by combining industry knowledge with company needs.

3. Create goals based on company values and mission statements; share them with your boss and the boss's boss.

4. If you have a boss block, document any poor interactions with them and be very careful who you trust with your venting.

5. Be loud, be bold.

Chapter 11: The fourth step on your journey to the C-suite

A large part of obtaining a seat at the table is getting noticed. A great way to do this is by creating a personal brand. Think of someone you admire. When I ask this, I often hear names like Michelle Obama, Oprah, Ruth Bader Ginsburg, Dwayne "The Rock" Johnson, or John Legend. Now if you think about these iconic individuals, they each have their own unique brand. Michelle Obama and John Legend are synonymous with a tailored wardrobe. You can't think of Oprah and Dwayne Johnson without picturing their thoughtful and expressive facial expressions and, of course, Ruth Bader Ginsburg and her famous lace collar.

Take a moment and to decide how you want to be viewed in the workforce. This can be easily accomplished by thinking of someone you admire and jotting down a few traits they possess. Think about how they conduct themselves under pressure. What are they wearing? What are their mannerisms? How are they speaking to others? These are branding traits you may want to consider adopting for yourself.

I am not suggesting be someone else, there is no point in that. You will only look disingenuous pretending to be something you're not. Rather, just consider how the person you admire might carry themselves in the workforce and try to emulate the traits you most admire in them. The goal is to present your best self at work.

A quick, solid way to establish a brand is through your wardrobe and appearance. More and more companies are adopting a work-from-home or jean-friendly work environment and that is great. But, the truth of the matter is, employers look at you differently when you dress more professionally. Studies have proven the way you dress will determine not only how seriously you are taken at work, but your wardrobe is also a large factor when you are being considered for promotion.

So, it is worth it to take the extra effort to tuck in your shirt and wear a belt. Or if on Zoom, do that hair and wear a nice shirt. Do your best to not only look your best, but also be your best and present.

I had a staff member who fought me on wardrobe for years. He claimed his work was and should be enough. "I'm always on time, I am reliable, and I provide great work. That should be sufficient," he would argue.

All of this was true, and I didn't deny that. He was one of the most trusted, talented, and reliable staff members I had. But he also disclosed to me in a yearly review it bothered him he wasn't "seen" by the executives.

"When we are onsite," he explained, "they (the executives) always pass right by me to ask you a question that has to do with my work. Although I'm standing right there, they will just walk by and ask you. You always have to come to me to get the answer, but that doesn't seem to stop them from passing me by to ask you. This happens all the time, and I don't get it. It makes me feel like I am invisible."

I couldn't argue with this, he was right, I had seen it happen many times, but I brought up an older conversation regarding his dress. Brad always dressed in cargo shorts or jeans with a black polo. This was not a bad casual look, but I suggested when in the office and onsite for events, maybe he should put in a little more effort with his wardrobe to stand out.

"You always say that," he rebutted. "It won't make a difference, you need to tell them to come to me."

There was no point explaining to him I already had. Instead, I made a bet with him.

"Ok, tell you what. I will tell the executives to come to you with questions, if you agree to dress a little better when we are onsite."

The conversation ended with Brad setting out to prove me wrong.

"Okay," he smirked, "I'll prove to you it's not that. At the next event, I'm going to wear a coat and tie and you will see, nothing will change." We shook on it, betting a hot coffee for the loser.

So, true to his word, at our next event Brad showed up on rehearsal day dressed in a very dashing coat and tie. His wardrobe became the hot topic of conversation for the remainder of the event. Everyone from hotel staff, his own crew, and the executive team commented again and again how nice he looked.

Guess what happened? When reviewing the stage environment, one of the executives had a question about where the steps were going in. When he turned to me, he stopped and looked around. When he saw Brad, he called him over asking us both his question. My coffee was delivered the very next morning by a humbled, yet nicely dressed employee.

Another example is a friend who had an important job interview on her horizon. The HR department of the well-known tech company told her to wear casual clothes to the interview and even went on to explain she would feel very out of place if she didn't.

I asked what she planned on wearing and wasn't surprised when she told me jeans and a T-shirt. After all, that's pretty much what they told her to wear. I implored her to wear something more professional. We argued about it for a while, and she insisted she didn't want to go against the grain and look like she didn't belong. I argued she also didn't want to blend into the interview pool.

Finally, she agreed to a shopping trip. I helped her pick out a nice professional pant outfit she didn't feel completely overdressed in, but clearly was not a "super casual" outfit by any means. She was confident wearing this to the interview was a mistake.

She called me from the parking lot after the meeting in tears and told me everyone looked at her funny. Some employees went as far as to tell her she was overdressed.

She pretty much accused me of costing her the job, and I have to tell you, I felt awful. Maybe it was outdated information I provided, perhaps I was wrong. I profusely apologized promising to never intervene with her career again.

She felt embarrassed and humiliated. And in the end, she felt completely employed because two days later they called her with an offer. Now let me say this, more than 200 candidates applied for her job. The odds are at least 10 percent of them were just as qualified and desired for the role.

So what set my friend apart? What made her memorable? It probably wasn't a nice outfit, but I'll just bet it didn't hurt her chances. Clearly, she stood out, and, let's face it, that was the goal.

Despite the evidence, research, and numerous articles written on this topic, this is typically a subject everyone wants to debate, so here is just one more example. My dear friend worked for a company for eight years without promotion. She complained to me she was overlooked and was considering looking for another job because, as she put it, she was "sick of it."

I recommended instead of putting a résumé together, we should try going shopping first. At the very worst, she would need a new interview suit, so she agreed. The following week, she returned to work wearing her new clothes. During a break at an onsite event, she called me.

"You won't believe this! The attendees are coming to me with questions and passing my boss. They think I'm in charge." She was elated, not just because the attendees were taking notice, but also because her boss's boss approached her for information. Even better, he did so in front of her boss. Joan never went to work in jeans again, even on Fridays and was promoted six months later.

I've provided enough examples, but because this the one topic I get the most push back on, I will not argue with anyone on this. I can only attest that I have seen it work over and over, not just for me, but many others as well. I have even gone as far as to brand my entire team.

We took this idea so seriously, we decided we would brand ourselves when we traveled together for site inspections and pre-conference meetings. We each carried the same computer bag (in our company's color) and wore a combination of pieces that matched. These included three blouses, a blazer, a pair of shoes, a scarf, and a sweater. When we traveled, we combined our like pieces with our personal choice of khaki pants, skirts, or shorts. We looked uniformed, branded, and presented ourselves as a unit receiving numerous compliments from vendors and our own leadership.

Your brand and appearance also matter in our virtual world. When you are attending a virtual meeting, please, please use your video. I realize that many of you will be told that you don't have to or that it's optional, but again here is another time when it matters.

Although you are told it's ok, consider how it looks each time you don't "show up". By just conducting the meeting with a screen with your name on it, you give the impression you are not really present. Yes, I'm sure you are hanging on every word and jotting notes, but unless you can be seen doing so, no one really knows you are. And if you are, you may as well get credit for it and the best way to get credit for being present at the meeting is to show up on video.

When attending, be sure to put effort into your appearance. Save the ball cap for non-video days.

As previously stated, this is a topic I will not argue about. The issue of dress tends to be a very personal matter and as the world changes, so should our ideas. Note I am not against dressing casually, and I'm certainly not against jeans. I just want to stress that a little more effort goes a long way. You already know it is my opinion that as event professionals, we have to work just a little harder than others to stand out.

Chapter recap.

1. Put in the effort with your appearance.

2. Use video on Zoom.

3. Dress for the promotion.

This step begins your journey to the C-suite. In the next few chapters we will explore some common pitfalls that contribute to our status. They are pitfalls and behaviors to avoid at all costs. They are also controversial, as every event planner seems to have their own set of ethics and guidelines for what is acceptable behavior. I will address my own personal tried, true, and tested code of ethics for how we as event professionals should behave on a day-to-day basis to be recognized as C-suite quality employees.

Chapter 12: You are not special, your job is

———————

Picture yourself as a VIP. You just arrived in Vegas after a fourteen-hour flight. You are tired. You want nothing more than to get to the hotel, get in your room, and take a quick shower.

You arrive at the airport and, although you were told a driver would meet you at baggage claim, no one is there. As you wait for your luggage, you look through your phone, searching for the email from the planner promising transportation. You call the number provided, but they do not answer. You hang up, gather your luggage, and make your way to the mile-long taxi line.

You stand in the Vegas heat wondering for a full half-hour what happened. During that time, you continue to dial the planner without the luck of reaching him. On the eighth call, you leave a message. When it is finally your turn for a cab, the driver announces the air conditioning is not operating and, as a result, you are forced to endure a breezy but not surprisingly hot ride to the hotel.

As you are unceremoniously dropped off at the hotel entrance, you gather your own luggage and enter the lobby. You remember reading you will have access to the VIP lounge for hotel check-in, but the security officer at the door regrets to inform you that you are not on the list. Embarrassed, you sigh and enter the long queue for the regular check-in.

Now you are clearly exhausted, confused, and a little peeved to be standing in a line, which doesn't seem to move. You take a moment to scan the lobby and see, just beyond the massive front doors, two members of your planning team. They are departing a limo and a representative of the hotel is there to greet them. They embrace in a hug and the hotel rep calls bellhops to assist with their luggage. The group is escorted into the hotel, and they disappear into the VIP lounge for check-in.

You finally have your hotel room key and are making your way down the massive hallway to your room when you spot the planning team and hotel contact just down the hall. You are close enough to see the team holding hotel-branded bottled water and carrying gift bags. The bellman props open the double doors to their room, working on transferring luggage from the cart to the foyer.

As you pass by, you look in curiously and catch a glimpse of a baby grand piano, huge windows overlooking the Las Vegas strip, a massive chandelier, and what looks to be a fully stocked wet bar. You overhear the hotel rep jokingly ask them if this luxury suite will do for their stay. Laughter from the group fills your ears as you finally reach your own hotel room.

You open your door and enter a standard run-of-house (ROH) room with two queen beds, although you specifically asked for a king room. You sigh dropping your things on one of the twin beds. Then curious about your own view slide open the heavy curtains only to be greeted with a view of the neighboring hotel's rooftop.

This is a true story! Astonishing as it sounds, it is true! How do you feel about the planning team? It's easy to put yourself in the position of the VP, isn't it? How likely do you think it is that the VP kept this story or their dissatisfaction to themselves? I can tell you they didn't and what happened next became a lose-lose situation for all involved.

The event team was pulled into a room by the CEO and told how embarrassed she was. The CEO demanded they move from the suite straight away and ensure the VP was moved into that suite. When the planners argued the suite was a four-bedroom and the hotel they were in was sold out, the CEO let them know she didn't care.

The event staff was sent to another hotel, given run-of-house rooms and forced to walk to the convention hotel each day for the remainder of the event. What a huge setback for our industry. Was it handled properly by the CEO? I can't say I condone that behavior either, but it was just so unnecessary! Had the planning team done their job of putting the VIPs and attendees first to begin with, this would have never happened.

Now you must know I am not saying it is never ok to accept the perks, quite the opposite. In fact, there are exactly two exceptions to agreeing to receive the gift without any complications.

1. You have made it to the C-suite and your title sanctions the upgrades and gifting.

2. You have been given permission from your leadership to accept the gifts.

That's it. How simple is that? In the example story above, had the event staff asked for permission to occupy the four-bedroom suite and been told "yes", then a completely different conversation would have happened. Certainly, one that included the importance of answering one's phone or checking to see if the VP could be upgraded. They more than likely would not have been made to leave the hotel.

Asking your leadership for permission is just good business sense. Chances are there is always someone they will want to take care of by floating them an extra perk like a larger room or complimentary transportation. Imagine the points you will score by suggesting a respected attendee or high-performing employee receive the complimentary hotel amenity or spa treatment. Serving your leadership and attendees should always be your primary goal.

If you are reluctant to ask leadership because you just know the answer is "no" before you even ask, then consider passing along a perk or two to a member of your Army before offering others to your leadership. Think of the brownie points you will obtain by floating over airport transportation or a room upgrade to one of these folks. The payoff is guaranteed and will last longer than any nights you spent in a suite.

Now I know that what I am proposing is not popular opinion. These perks have typically been part of the charm of our job, and we all want and deserve to be taken care of. But I will stress this again, unless you are in the C-suite it is just better for you to pass these perks along or politely decline. Don't fool yourself. Leadership and attendees do notice your table is receiving a better class of wine, and they see that hotel employee handing you a vanilla latte each morning.

You are mistaken if you think these perks are not contributing to the belief we are not C-suite material, and if you think leadership or attendees don't care because they don't say anything, you are incorrect. I promise you this topic keeps being brought to my attention by various members of leadership again and again. It's critical to our profession that we hold ourselves to a higher standard if we want to be viewed as C-suite material.

Let's discuss for a moment other types of gifting like concert tickets, T-shirts, trips to visit hotels. Because ethics is a very fine line, I've included the most common examples of perks and shared a handy OK / NOT OK list as it pertains to vendor gifting and favors.

SITUATION:

Hotel gifts you with branded items (blankets, bags, robe, socks, etc.) or sends food to your room during an event or site inspection.

OK or NOT OK?

Answer: Mostly ok

Why

You are conducting business with the hotel. You are either in the middle of the event or on a site post a signed contract. This can get a bit iffy if you haven't signed a contract. If you do not plan on using the hotel, you will need to use your best judgment if the gift you are provided is acceptable. If it is a small token of appreciation, you are fine. If they are giving you expensive gifts and you have no intention of bringing business to the location, then it's probably best to decline the offer.

SITUATION:

You're planning a vacation with the family, and you use your title to request a suite upgrade, free night stay, or free meal.

OK or NOT OK

Not ok

Why not ok

Even if you have previously held an event there or have a contract to use the hotel for a future event, asking a vendor to gift you anything is unethical. The contact will give you complimentary rooms at the hotel for the use of the site inspection, they are not obligated to gift you a vacation based on a contract you're not even paying to fulfill. Even if you are personally shelling out the cost of the contract, your vendors are in the business to make money and handing out freebies costs them.

Put yourself in their shoes, you have probably had a friend, co-worker, or boss asks you to use your industry contacts to obtain favors. They call during your busy day to see if they can get free tickets, hotel stays, a suite upgrade, or to ask for a reservation at that new hip restaurant that is packed for the next six months. They expect you to drop everything and fit in some time to handle their request. And you know deep down, it's not going to happen for them. Multiply that feeling times about a thousand and now you know what it's like on the vendor side when you ask. The odds of you being the only call that day are unlikely.

SITUATION:

You are on vacation at a property where you have a signed contract or have conducted business and request complimentary food or beverage be sent to your room.

OK or NOT OK

Not ok

Why not ok

If you have signed a contract, keep in mind it's not your money. The company you represent signed the contract not you, and therefore it is the company's.

I recently sat down with a hotel vendor friend of mine who told me a couple of stories about planners coming forward asking for free hotel rooms right after the Covid-19 pandemic. This was a very unfortunate time in our industry's history, and hotels were forced to lay off and furlough hundreds of thousands of our fellow hospitality workers.

The ask for a freebie wasn't at all taken lightly in consideration of those who lost their jobs. Think about the climate of the industry and know a little about the health of your vendors before suggesting upgrades, free nights, and food. Or better yet, stay clear of asking for favors altogether. It's just not a good look.

Now let's say your vendor insists. This is highly probable because our vendors do love to spoil us, so if they just won't take no for an answer and tell you they really want you to have an expensive gift, etc. Well, this is an entirely different matter. If you experience this, then know that you have recruited a member of your Army. Great job and accept away.

Regardless, it is critically important that you hold a candid conversation with your leadership regarding what is and is not acceptable. I've heard horror stories where planners new to a company just accepted gifting like they had in previous roles only to find later that they were in violation of the companies ethics policy and dismissed from their job. It is extremely important to know the expectations of your employer and act accordingly. If you find that your company does not have a set of guidelines, well then, you have an amazing opportunity to show your leadership skills by creating one. At the end of the day, just use your best judgment in these matters. Look at your vendor relationships as partnerships. You don't blatantly take advantage of your partner do you? At least I hope not.

Upgrades and gifting are just the tip of the ethics iceberg, so in the next chapter we will dive down into the icy waters to explore the bottom half to ensure we have examined ethics in their entirety.

Chapter 13: Ethical AF

As we established there are lots of definitions out there about what is and isn't acceptable regarding gifting and perks in our industry. I am of the mindset that how we handle these situations as a whole will have a lasting effect on our reputation and the belief that ours is just a fun party job not deserving of a leadership title. I've outlined a few topics I receive the most questions on when helping professionals on their journey to the C-suite.

Hotel Reward Points:

It is my personal belief these should not be provided to an individual. Instead, it is a much better value prop to show these are being held in a company pool, either for charity, employee travel, or perhaps site inspections.

Now, I have run into some circumstances where the hotels will not put them in a company name and require it to be an individual. In this instance, a larger conversation needs to be had with your leadership on their preference. Stop for a moment and consider what a conversation like this will mean for your reputation.

Hey boss, I stand to gain 150,000 hotel points for this contract, but I do not believe these should come to me personally. I mean, it is not my money that is paying for the event. So, instead, I think we should recycle these for the Special Olympics or maybe use them for employee incentives or on our next site inspection.

This is a very big deal. It shows you are mindful of company money and seeking ways to add to the value proposition. Hmmm, sounds like you might be thinking like a leader. If you own your own event company, this can be easily accomplished and the points used to gift your top clients or staff.

Now, it may surprise you to know I do not feel the same about airline points. I believe those should be kept and used by you. This is a perk for spending time away from your family and friends and should be used at your discretion.

Site Inspections:

Site inspections are not vacations. If they were, then they would be called vacations. But they're not, they are called site inspections. They are work. You should get in and out with a heavy itinerary to view all you need to make your decision. Your husband, your mother, your father, your sister, or your best friend has no business being there. You should be up early and in bed late with a full agenda to occupy your days.

If you have been doing your job for a while with the same company, you can pretty much walk into a place and know within seconds if the venue is going to work or not. If you're new with a company, this will take a little more time, but one truth is clear: if you are the type of person who gets upset when your feet are sore, you tire easily, or you get back pain from standing up all day, this is not a profession for you.

Know the general idea from people outside our profession is site inspections are some type of fun break. I personally love it when I hear from my clients that their boss demands to come on the site, only to complain and ask exhaustedly, "Are all site inspections like this one?" Yes, yes, they are because they are not a vacation.

A great story about such a boss comes from my friend Louise. She reported to a new boss who, when they found out what a site inspection was, (because the new boss had no prior event experience) just had to join Louise on the very next one, which happened to be in Nashville.

Leading up to travel, Louise would tell me that she overheard her asking staff what she should pack and discussing bars in the area that would be fun to visit. Despite Louise sharing the travel agenda with her, she just knew her new boss wasn't prepared for the trip. It was obvious she was under the common impression that site inspections are mini-breaks and that was more obvious than when she arrived at the airport in strappy heels.

They landed in Nashville and began the site visit immediately. First on the list, the convention center followed by two hotels before checking into their host hotel. Mid-convention center tour and only about an hour into the day, her new boss began to whine she was getting tired and her feet hurt.

Louise was embarrassed and also a little worried knowing the group still had two hotels to visit before the first stop. Well, she was right to be worried because while the group was inspecting a run-of-house room at the first hotel, the new boss took it upon herself to sit on the bed. A huge no-no! You are there to examine the room, not to check-in! The last thing housekeeping wants to hear is a call to clean a room because some lazy, unschooled planner sat on the bed. It's not only lazy, it is also rude.

When the inspection of the first hotel ended and the group stood in the lobby waiting for transportation to pull around, the new boss actually removed her shoes and began rubbing her feet right out in the open public area. Louise distanced herself from her boss by moving to the opposite end of the lobby, not wanting anyone to know she was with her. She prayed that would be the last of her embarrassing antics, but some prayers go unanswered.

When they arrived at the second hotel, the new boss stated she actually had stayed there before and, as a result didn't need to see the hotel. She opted to sit in the lobby. Louise could not have been more apologetic to her hotel contact. Post tour, the group headed to the host hotel to check-in. They agreed to take thirty minutes before meeting back in the lobby to continue the site inspection of a few off-site farewell reception locations.

A half-hour later, Louise was in the hotel lobby attempting to reach her new boss by phone while she apologized to her destination management company (DMC) contact for running twenty minutes behind schedule. Yes, the new boss was impacting the remainder of the appointments and times by showing up a half-hour late for part two of their day. The new boss remained in the air conditioned van for two of the four off-site site locations and only perked up when the DMC contact announced he would be treating the group to a nice steak dinner at a local restaurant before returning them to the hotel for the evening.

During the meal when the new boss excused herself to the restroom, the DMC contact leaned over to Louise and asked her why the she was over the department and not Louise. He noticed she didn't seem to understand the point of the site and wasn't engaged in the process,

"She doesn't appear to know what she is doing," he confided.

Truth be told, Louise should have been elated. Finally someone else was seeing what she knew all along! But later she confessed to me the comment left her profoundly sad.

"He struck a nerve about what I'd been thinking for some time." She told me, "Why WASN'T I in charge of the event department?"

I didn't have an answer for her. Clearly, she had the knowledge, skill, and professionalism, so what was the problem? The thought stuck with Louise and then really bothered her when new boss pulled her next stunt. After dinner, the new boss realizing the group didn't have anything else planned, and asked the DMC contact to take the group to a nearby bar she had read about.

Ok, so this is usually the time in the site visit when Louise and her team would retire to the hotel to compare notes. Nope, the new boss wanted to go out, so the DMC extended the use of the company car and accompanied them to the watering hole.

Suddenly the new boss had a surge of energy and wasted no time ordering tequila shots for the group. Louise and her team politely declined the drink as they, like her, had to be up for one of those famous red-eye flights at 3:00 a.m. the following morning. The new boss apparently was not one to waste alcohol and graciously accepted the shots for the group.

Soon after her third shot, the bar announced the mechanical bull was in operation. This was clearly Louise's cue to leave but not the new boss. No, she suggested everyone take a turn. Again Louise and her team declined, but the new boss jumped up and hopped right on. Louise and the team were treated to quite the spectacle when the mechanical bull operator caused the bull to lean the new boss forward and then shake her from side to side, jiggling her breasts at the crowd of onlookers.

Louise was red with embarrassment but the new boss loved it, throwing her head back in laughter. "This is my 'superior'?" Louise thought. "This is a person who is being fast-tracked at the company to senior VP?"

Trust me, I know Louise and she is all in for a good time, but not when she is representing her company. On top of it, the poor DMC contact was on his personal time now and for what? So, the boss could let loose? Not the time or place!

Site inspections are necessary to verify location and get a sense of surroundings before making a decision on a program. I'm not saying don't stop to smell the roses, but don't pause and crush a bottle of tequila, especially in front of your vendors/partners.

Conduct yourself as a professional and come to the site prepared to work. Do some homework on the centers and venues, and, above all, be respectful of your vendor's time. If you are running late, be sure to let them know. Take lots of photos and make lots of notes. The more details you jot down, the better off you will be when trying to remember the room you want for a certain event or which to avoid.

It's a good idea to share the program agenda with venue staff before arrival. Note any special needs a function may have, such as a nice view, stage, location close to the general session, etc.

The contact knows the venue better than you and can assist with your desires, even if the room you want wasn't in the contract to begin.

Another good idea is to share your site inspection agendas with leadership before you travel. Arm them with your intended agenda, so they can see firsthand how your time will be spent. When you return, be sure to provide a written recap on your findings as well as any details that benefited you seeing the location.

For instance, that great looking boardroom with all the windows just happened to be located next to a rather large construction site and because you were there, you were able to negotiate a move to a more peaceful location. Use real photos from your travels to illustrate the true representation of the location and not the pretty photoshopped photos used online. Educating leadership is a critical factor in helping them understand the importance of seeing sites before program dates.

Family and Friends traveling with you during an active event:

We established friends and family should not travel on-site inspections, but this also rings true for active events. You are working. Just because you are working in another city, does not mean you are not required to be on call 24/7 in the event of any emergency. Friends and family are a distraction.

Case in point, Sandy was an unschooled planner who tried to convince an industry buddy of mine she should be allowed to bring her family to events. She told my friend Brad it wasn't a distraction for them to come, and she was able to complete her job just fine with them present. Brad and I discussed this at length, as he and I are on the same page and in agreement you don't take your family to the office and the same is true for events.

Please know, I am all about extending one's stay in any destination after event completion. I also agree and speak to leaders to support giving planners extra personal days to detox with family or friends after an event. I also advocate hotel group rates should be afforded to planning staff for up to seven nights after the event.

But as for family onsite during the time planners should be working, well that is not a good look. Our jobs onsite are too demanding, and there are too many times we are called upon to troubleshoot and focus on a situation we didn't anticipate. Having friends and family in the wings waiting for your time and attention can be complicated. The truth is we have no idea of the obstacles that await us when we arrive onsite. Even in a virtual world, we must keep ourselves 100 percent focused and available 24/7 for the task at hand.

Nevertheless, Sandy argued with Brad that her family came with her ALL the time and they had NEVER been a distraction. In an attempt to placate Sandy, Brad offered her some non-PTO (personal time off), so she could extend her trip and bring in her family after the event. But Sandy wasn't having it. Apparently, she had already told her daughter and her daughter's friend they could come to California, and they were already packed.

So, Brad and I discussed this at length and he decided, against his better judgment and because he was new in his role and didn't want to come across as some kind of a jerk, to allow Sandy to bring her daughter and her daughter's friend. He even took it a step further and gave the trio his corner room, so they would have more space for their group. At this point, he was thinking, "Who knows, maybe I'm wrong and Sandy found a way to bring people without them getting in the way."

Spoiler alert, she did not.

The first order of business upon arrival at the hotel was pre-con. It was the typical twenty-person hollow square pre-con with the general manager and all department heads. You know, busy people. They were about ten minutes into the meeting when Sandy's phone rang and, ready for this? She takes the call. What a great message to the twenty hotel department heads who took time out of their busy day to be present.

"Hello, honey," Sandy cooed, not even having the courtesy to step away from the table. "I have a key, how come yours isn't working?"

Meanwhile, Brad is staring around the room, wide-eyed in horror.

"Well, calm down. Just come get mine, we are in the hibiscus room on, hold on . . ." She pulled the phone away and asked the room, "What floor are we on?"

"Third," the general manager replied.

Sandy continued, "We're on the third floor, yes, hibiscus. H, I, B, I, no B, not C. Honey, stop, listen to me, okay, are you ready? H, I, B as in boy, I, S, C as in cactus, U, S... got it? Okay, see you soon."

She puts the phone next to her.

"Where were we?" someone says.

Then, about thirty minutes into the meeting, there is a knock on the door. Sandy gets up without excusing herself or apologizing and opens the door wide enough to expose her daughter and friend, standing there wrapped in hotel towels with dripping wet hair. They proceed to discuss the key for some time.

Then, she turns to the pre-con attendees and asks the front desk manager if she can replace the faulty key during this meeting. The manager complies by radioing the front desk for someone to join her in the room with a new key.

Brad told me he just wanted to crawl under the table. Not only is she representing the company he worked for, but she was also representing him. "How is this not a distraction?" he would later yell into the phone at me as we discussed her behavior.

The three-day event continued with Sandy inviting her daughter and her daughter's friend to a dinner sponsored by the hotel. Brad and I both agreed that was rather tacky. Why did the hotel need to pay for the two of them? It was a nice gesture for them to invite Brad and Sandy, but to bring the family along was taking advantage. I'm sad to report, the antics didn't stop there.

The evening of the closing reception, Sandy approached Brad to announce she was taking off, as she had promised the girls dinner in town with it being their last night and all. Brad looked around at the still very busy ballroom and replied he thought that was an interesting choice considering the reception had not yet concluded. He suggested a new plan, which required her to stay to the end to be on the job in the event her services were needed.

Her adult response was to huff, turn on her heel, and join a group of her friends at the bar for another glass of wine. This was her contribution to staying and helping close the reception.

When the reception did end, she stormed past Brad as he called out to her, "Have a good night and be safe." She either didn't hear or ignored him. We still don't know for sure.

Needless to say, Brad never allowed Sandy to bring family to an event again. He wrote down the full incident and was thankful for doing so when his boss called him in to tell him she had lodged a complaint to leadership claiming Brad was too strict. When Brad was able to speak to the incident, the complaint was dismissed. Sandy quit sometime after this, and he was able to replace her with a professional planner whose priorities and personal life were in the right place.

Vendor Relationships:

Another item to note here critical to being not only an ethical professional but a good human being is to not blame vendors for your mistakes.

A friend of mine worked an event where the CEO was planning to present each member of the leadership team with a $200 gift card as thank you for their service. A member of the marketing team ordered these directly and had them branded with the event logo as a continued reminder of the time spent together.

Well, that same team member entered the wrong address when placing the order, which resulted in the cards being delivered to a sister property about seven hours away from where the actual event took place. To make matters worse, the mistake was discovered late in the day the cards were to be delivered to the attendees' rooms. There was no way these cards were getting to the right hotel in time.

Cyndi was in the staff office when she overhead the members of the marketing team begin brainstorming solutions to the problem. For them, the priority was not so much how to rectify the issue but rather how to spin the story, so the person who made the mistake wouldn't be held accountable. She overhead the conversation and listened as they prattled on about how they were going to get out of this.

Cyndi interrupted to suggest they simply tell the CEO the truth. She suggested at the end of their event, which was concluding the following day, they work to retrieve the branded gift cards from the other hotel and mail them to each attendees' homes after the conference with a nice handwritten from the CEO note thanking them for attending. It wasn't a far-fetched idea since their CEO had already planned to write handwritten thank you notes anyway.

"Package the gift cards with the note in something like an event wrap-up kit. This will also serve as a reminder of what was learned during the conference and of our time together," she said.

The group seemed to pause for a long while before the person who made the error said flatly, "No, I don't want to do that."

They went back to their discussion. Cyndi frankly was stunned. Seeking clarity, she asked, "But didn't you say that the cards at the other hotel are branded to our event?"

"Yeah, so?"

"So, it's doubtful we can return them. If we can't return them, isn't that a big waste of money?" She quickly calculated that at $200 per attendee times 300 attendees, this amounted to $60,000.

"Yeah, but that isn't the focus right now," her co-worker argued and the team continued to brainstorm a solution for an additional hour.

What was their brilliant solution to this problem? First, blame the vendor that shipped them. They informed the CEO the vendor sent the gift cards to the wrong hotel. He seemed disappointed and they matched that sentiment, "I know, we are so upset with them!"

Although tempted to tell the truth, Cyndi kept quiet.

Then the marketing team sent three members of the event planning team out to nearby drug and grocery stores in the area to physically purchase 300 more $200 gift cards. This process took about five hours in total with some of them even running into each other at the same store (eye roll here).

Funny how the event team was deemed the perfect group to be sent on the errand mid-event, but I digress.

In the end, instead of receiving a card with the event logo and conference branding, attendees received a hodgepodge of generic gift cards from various credit card companies. Not to mention the man-hours wasted on going out to physically pick up the cards. The event was very much in full swing when they sent three members of the planning team on the impromptu scavenger hunt for a product that had already been purchased.

Cyndi and I had a hard time wrapping our minds around that logic. I remember her telling me about this over cocktails one night after work. "So, what did you learn from this?" I asked her blankly.

"That I'm allergic to stupid," she replied, not missing a beat.

She never did find out what happened to the $60,000 investment in the pre-printed cards sent to the wrong hotel. I encouraged her to bring it up with leadership, but she felt so conflicted she dropped it and started to look for another job.

This story had an impact on me, and I began to think about all the times I've been aware of event professionals blaming the vendor for mistakes they made. Frankly, it is too easy. We are human and we will screw up, but if you can think back to a time when you were blamed for something you didn't do, you can easily recall how frustrating it is, even hurtful.

It's important to understand your vendors are an extension of the team. They are essential to the success of the event and should be treated accordingly. Include your vendors in team events like staff meals, planning meetings, and post-celebrations. Your vendors can be long-lasting friends and Army members who help navigate your career, choices, and give you company and industry insight that can be instrumental to your success. Pushing undue blame in their direction will damage your company's reputation, but more importantly, it will totally ruin your own.

I realize it is very hard to admit when you are wrong and almost more so for event professionals, as nearly every aspect of your job is dissected and scrutinized throughout the entire planning process. It's no surprise everyone has an opinion and feels entitled to share it. But admitting fault is part of ethics. It's more important to troubleshoot, correct the issue, and show what you did to overcome it than to point at an easy target.

So, I encourage you to do just that. It is more likely you will uncover your mistake long before anyone else. Take a moment, breathe, troubleshoot, involve members of your Army, if necessary, and correct it. Then, when all is said and done, make leadership aware of what happened and how you managed the issue. Yes, it really is that easy.

The ethical discussion is not new, but it is important. Our career should be very important to us and the actions we take today will have a long-lasting effect on our profession for years to come. We have such a unique role, and it is often misunderstood. To others, it looks so glamorous, fun, and exciting. To us, we often feel underappreciated, overworked, and misunderstood. We have to work to keep our own spirits up, too often we are our own cheerleaders.

In the next chapter, I will share tips on how to objectively evaluate your work. We will also explore techniques to share your value without coming across as you are complaining or boasting.

Chapter 14: Logic vs. emotion, learn to love feedback

Here is a secret. This job is personal. It just is. We spend way too much of our lives, our thoughts, and our time on our careers. It is important to us, and therefore it is personal. Whoever says otherwise is certainly not an event planner. To say "it's just business" is sarcastic and, honestly, a little spiteful. I picture a mob boss with a gun to his enemy's head saying, "Hey kid, it's just business," before pulling the trigger.

This is your reputation, your life, and, in many ways, your identity. Event professionals are artists. Have you ever known an artist? Fun, eccentric, and often larger than life. We create; our canvas is the event and we sculpt experiences. It should be no surprise we take it to heart when people act as critics and diminish our pets. Especially when they give us non-productive feedback.

But here is the problem, executives and C-suite level employees tend to lean on the logical non-emotional side of matters. When is the last time you have seen your CFO cry at work? Executives don't tend to hyper-defend their work, whine, point fingers, or get emotional. So, to adopt that leadership trait, we must strive to make our day-to-day decisions and interactions all about business.

A perfect starting point to achieve this is to become comfortable with feedback and criticism. We must stop defending every and any negative feedback we receive, whether it be written or verbal. I don't know why attendees feel obligated to let us know every single little thing that upset them while attending our conference, but I do know that their consistent badgering isn't going to change. We have to work to change how we react to it.

My first recommendation in presenting ourselves in a logical and non-emotional manner is to alter the way we ask for and receive event feedback. Look, you are always going to get someone's opinion whether you ask for it or not, so you may as well take steps to identify the trash evaluation from quality suggestions.

Start by creating a decent post-event survey to aid you and your team in making genuine improvements for the following year. I have never been a fan of, and stay away from, asking a post-event survey question not designed to help us improve in the long run.

For example, if I cannot improve the food quality or guarantee I can, I try to stay away from that as a question on the survey. Instead, I might ask about the offerings. Did attendees feel there were enough options to meet their dietary needs? You can bank on receiving the comment that the food was crappy, but, much like heating and air, that is really beyond our control.

This is the reason I'm not a fan of tastings. I don't see the point in asking my vendor to have their chef prepare a free meal, so I can sample the dinner I'll be serving for the gala, award ceremony, president's dinner, what have you. It doesn't take a Harvard degree to know that cooking for a small group of no more than five people is significantly different than cooking for 4,000.

Also, I've been around to know how chicken cordon bleu will look, smell, and taste coming from a banquet kitchen. Can we please stop wasting our vendor's time?

Now here is where you say, well, the food quality is really important to my group and I have to taste to ensure that it's the quality cut, size, and freshness they expect. To that I say rubbish. Instead, I recommend a simple sit-down with the culinary staff to describe your needs. Make them part of the team by asking about their suppliers and whether the menu you selected is ideal for the time of year the event will take place. The best thing you can do for yourself and them is ask what they recommend based on your budget. I have yet to have staff attempt to upsell me on something I can't afford, and some of the best meals I've had were due to these conversations. Give the kitchen staff the ability to blow you away by inviting them to the conversation and planning process without having to take time out of their day to fry you a fish. I promise, they won't disappoint.

Another question to stay away from is the comfort of meeting rooms. It's irrelevant, you can't go back in time and change it, so don't even address it. Don't worry about not asking, because they will find a place on the survey to include it. Since there isn't anything you can do about it, this is garbage feedback. We can and do ask venues all day to keep the room temperature at 71 degrees. We have spent a good number of hours relaying on our two-way radios to our venue contact that a room is too hot, too cold, too hot, too cold. We have even walked the space to check the temperature ourselves before any event begins. It's never right, so stop worrying about it.

Now, I'm not suggesting you don't worry about it onsite. Of course, do that. But post event, there is not a damn thing you can do about it, so that feedback is useless. You already know it's going to be a struggle for next time, and there is nothing to be learned from complaints about the temperature. Although we can sympathize when someone is too hot or too cold, we are not licensed mechanics no matter how much attendees expect us to be.

Now, to obtain relevant feedback that is business-oriented and not emotional, it's essential to ask the right questions. Questions based on logic. Only then can you create a post-event report discussing where ROI was hit, where it was lacking, and what improvements you have already implemented as a result of previous feedback. If you are sending the survey, then you have the luxury of receiving the results before leadership. Use that to your advantage by removing emotional jargon that cannot be corrected such as too hot, too cold, cold chicken breast, rain, etc.

If you have a lot of responses and content, a good idea is to divide the results among your team to review and report back. Look for consistency across the team. Maybe someone caught something others didn't; maybe someone interpreted feedback differently. Make the dissection of the feedback a team effort and keep an open mind. Weed through the trash, then weed again, then weed one last time. Now it is ready for executive-level communication. Be careful not to inundate your executive team, they typically bore easily.

If used correctly, feedback can be an excellent tool for getting your seat at the table. If something was screwed up that was your responsibility and noticed by more than a few attendees, own it. These are things like there wasn't enough signage in the common areas, or the help desk wasn't manned during the operating hours, or the dress code changed and wasn't covered in all communications.

Do not shy away from mistakes; you can only guarantee they will not happen again. Do not beat yourself up and do not allow others to beat you up either. Make a note and move on.

My friend Tara used to throw herself a brief pity party at her desk when she made a minor error. She would open a fictional desk drawer and pretended to toss confetti in the air, then pretend to sweep it up and return the imaginary confetti to the invisible drawer before shutting it and putting the incident behind her. By confronting and acknowledging your mistakes, you are also building trust with your leadership. It's uncomfortable, but it is a massive step illustrating your professional maturity.

Once you and your team have thoroughly dissected the feedback, create a quick and easy-to-read report. Include what worked, what didn't, which speakers had high marks, and which didn't. If there are improvements to be made, illustrate in the report how you intend to address these for next time. If you can share with leadership in a meeting, do so. If they are "too busy," send an email and request follow-up. If you do not receive any feedback, set a calendar reminder for a week and send another request. Keep at it, this is important.

Mind you, I have worked for some amazingly bad leaders. If you find yourself in a position where you are afraid to admit the mistake because they are unusually harsh, then it's time to reassess your worth and try to get out of that environment before they start to mess with your confidence.

I know all too well the price you will pay mentally if you remain in that culture. It is easy enough to recognize. Your co-workers have probably already tossed you under the bus in several incidences and leadership didn't bother to ask your side of the story. I know it's not easy to find a job or start at a new company, especially as an event professional, but you be clear with yourself you are worth more than this.

On the opposite end, let's say you become or are an executive within a toxic environment. My advice is to stay humble and be a servant leader. You may not be able to control all the negativity for everyone employed, but you can still protect and grow your team. I've had leaders like this, and they forever hold a place in my heart.

Another hot point that can cause some serious emotional distress is one we already know is going to happen for every event. It's the call to the head office when someone finally decides to look at all the communications you have been sending for the past few months. This is typically one-to-two weeks before the event, and now because they are paying attention, they want to change almost everything. From speaker line-ups to training start and end times, breaks, and dinner dates. Believe it or not, I've even had to change the theme of this close-to-go date.

Now the gut reaction is to stare at them blankly then scream "What a half-witted suggestion! Just how simpleminded are you?" and proceed to wave our hands about, continuing with a long lecture on exactly the man-hours we have put in, the number of communications already sent, and the laundry list of what it is going to take to make their changes.

While this might make us feel better, it's not exactly C-Suite behavior. So, no matter how much we would like to berate them and no matter how much they deserve it, it's best to take a deep breath, make notes of the "suggested" changes, and then use the Time, Quality, and Cost module.

If you have not used it, it's a common module demonstrating how a change to a nearly completed project will have an immediate impact on one, two, or all of the components of time, quality, or cost. Based on the suggestions, you should be able to pinpoint and logically discuss with this person the impact on the bottom line.

For instance, say they want to add a speaker, but you don't have time on the general session agenda. You can show adding the speaker will impact all three aspects of the time, quality, and cost module. You will be over budget with the addition of the speaker's fee, accommodations, and transportation. Quality will suffer because, in order to make time for the speaker to present, all others will need to decrease their stage time. If the program runs late, the room can't be set in time for dinner, so it may need to be pushed back, and since the final outline was due to the vendor, they will most likely charge a change fee, etc., etc., etc.

Other examples of these changes may include your printed and digital materials. Suppose these are final at the time agenda changes are requested. Because they are in final production it will cost (insert price here) to be reformatted and cost (insert price here) for a developer to change the App.

Perhaps scriptwriters will need to adjust the run-of-show. Or your team will need to discontinue work to complete other aspects of the event, focus on the changes, and re-visit communications to the presenters for the general session.

It's possible graphics will need to be updated, and the venue knows break times have changed to ensure food isn't sitting out long enough to spoil, making people sick. The list of potential impacts goes on and on depending on the changes made.

Using the Time, Quality, and Cost module helps you speak logically about the changes and potentially lessen the urge to throw something at their head. Disclaimer: I said, "could".

In time, you will learn to embrace when someone wants to make some pretty significant changes at the last minute. Their suggestions can provide a great opportunity to highlight the work you and your team have done to that point to ensure a successful event. Think of the satisfaction you will have when you can provide them with a little peek behind the curtain, so they can see first-hand all the steps needed to be taken to accommodate the one seemingly tiny request they just made. Like a light bulb going off, you will see a transition happen as they grasp and truly understand the amount of work your team have done.

I've found the more these conversations happened, the less inclined they were to demand last-minute updates. It was an interesting transition. True enough, in the beginning, it was hard to have these conversations. My palms would sweat and I'd turn red, but the more confident I remained, keeping my points professional, matter of fact, and logical, the more comfortable I became. As a result, I was more trusted by leadership and their last-minute request became non-existent. Practice makes perfect.

The point is not to shy away from the conversation by saying, "Ok, we can do that," and then cry in the bathroom questioning how in the hell you are going to make it all happen. Come to the meeting prepared to be blown away with the suggestions, but also bring a copy of the Time, Quality, and Cost model. Because let's face it, you know you are going to need it.

With all of this talk about last-minute changes and surveys, I have failed to mention a very important component before you depart for the event. That is the pre-event meeting. About two weeks before show time, call a meeting that enables you to set expectations, discuss the flow of the event, and any last-minute details you wish to share. Invite just about anyone who is anyone and can attend: speakers, key members of your production team, leadership, and key staff.

Remember to schedule this meeting well in advance before your attendees' calendars become jam-packed. Send weekly reminders leading up to the meeting and highlight a few key items you will discuss to entice them, so they won't reschedule you. Revisit the mission statement and company values, making your points correlate with them. Use bullet points to communicate. If they want to discuss a topic further, they will ask more questions.

The point of the meeting is inclusion and zombification. Remember the majority of your communications go unread, and you will spend a good amount of time resending emails to attendees who will claim they didn't receive anything from you. An in-person meeting outlining some key need-to-know details goes a long way.

Now, I understand organizing and conducting these meetings won't work with all leadership teams. Some are just ego-driven dictators who bark orders and do not care to hear what you have to say. They are also the ones who are surprised when things go poorly or over budget.

I once was told of a company where the leadership was notorious for bringing the planning groups together to belittle them after the event. They would call a meeting and pick apart every little thing that they perceived went wrong, and when someone tried to defend the reason, they were screamed at. If you find yourself in this type of situation, there is nothing more you can do than to sharpen your résumé and start actively looking elsewhere.

The ultimate goal here is to get to the C-suite, so you can have a direct impact as a member of the leadership team and promote quality change. The best way to do that is to be at the top of your game, educated, branded, professional, and logical.

Chapter recap

1. Set up a pre-event meeting with leadership to review expectations and program flow.

2. Spend time with survey results to create a post-event executive report.

3. Try to deliver results in person but create a stellar post-event report if you are unable to do so.

4. Illustrate lessons learned and plans to improve for the future. Come with solutions to problems.

5. Admit mistakes if needed, but also point out what was learned.

6. Work on removing yourself from toxic environments.

Now let's talk about the most important aspect of your career; yourself.

Chapter 15: Know your worth

You are educated, ethical, have created some new processes, and delivered some pretty kick-ass experiences. If the company you are working for doesn't listen to your ideas, or allow you to implement them, passes you up for promotion, or rewards low performers, then it is time you move on. The key is knowing what an amazing resource you are. Any company would greatly benefit from your knowledge and professionalism, and you deserve to be treated with respect.

Finding a new job is a lot like dating. You go online looking for what seems to be a great fit, put yourself out there, and often don't hear squat. I could write an entire book on how flawed the job search process is. It's heartbreaking, demeaning, and cruel. If you ever want to test your self-esteem, just try to find a new job. But, it is and remains a necessary evil, so below is my quick guide on how to navigate the stormy waters of job hunting.

Invest in your online profile before sending any resumes. Be sure your social media outlets are free from political statements, photos of you and your friends in the club, or any other questionable content. If you don't think they are looking, you're wrong.

Spend time with professional social media outlets. Select a nice headshot, complete all profile settings and spend more time with your self-description. This profile can be the catalyst that sets you apart from other applicants, so be sure it is on point.

Purchase a resume template and update it as necessary. Have an editor review it or send it to lots of friends and family for input. You want to stand apart from the competition, and the overall look of your resume will help achieve that goal.

After those steps, you are ready to start applying. Commit to sending at least five resumes each week. If you find more jobs of interest, that is great. But I stress - you should be selective and picky. The end goal is to become a valued member of the right organization, not jumping from one toxic environment to the next.

Be patient. It has become a sad and, for lack of a better word, gross trend that HR event "professionals" now ghost applicants. I have had many friends tell me they had a great phone interview only to never hear from the company again...EVER. It's rude and lazy, but it's the trend.

I once read a post to a reply a candidate wrote complaining about this very topic in which the replier wrote "get over it, these people don't owe you anything." Headshaking that we live in a society were common curtesy should not be expected.

I also don't get why they can't tell you exactly why you didn't get the role. You must understand when starting the process so many decisions on who they hire have very little, if anything, to do with you. For instance, they may be required by law to post a job when they already know who they will hire for the role, wasting your time and theirs because they have to show they interviewed other candidates. This happens quite a bit and the entire process can wear you down, making it very hard to stay positive.

As you cast your fishing pole into the job pond and wait for a nibble, use the time to perfect your phone interview skills. Most likely the first step to securing a face-to-face interview will be a phone interview with HR. Do some research on typical questions asked during these initial conversations and have a friend work with you on practicing.

The goal of the phone interview with HR should be to advance to the second stage. Find out from this person the process for hiring. Most typically, it's a phone interview with HR, followed by a face-to-face (often online) interview with the hiring manager. From there it may be another interview with their boss or even their team, your future co-workers. During each phase, the interview usually becomes more detailed. In your initial HR interview, it's best to keep your attitude upbeat and questions general. They are simply trying to determine if they want to work with you. If they do, you will advance to the next step.

When you do advance to the next step in the interview, now is the time to do some research on the company. Visit not only the company's website, but also search for past employee reviews of the company's leadership and culture. Be prepared to show you have basic knowledge of the leadership, company mission statement, and how you can contribute to achieving company goals.

Keep in mind that you are also interviewing the company. The road to employment is a two-way street. They will drill you to decide if you are a good fit, but you owe it to yourself to do the same to prevent yourself from jumping from one bad environment to another.

As discussed in a previous chapter, the job description may not always match the job. To ensure that this company will not only be a good fit for you but also you will be happy with the work, I've provided a few key questions to ask your future employer and aid you in determining if this company is a good match. These questions should be asked of your hiring manager.

1.   Why is this role vacant?

•   You are trying to get to the bottom of what happened to the person who had the job before you. If they quit, that could be a red flag. However, if they retired, moved, won the lottery, or the role is newly created, then these are perfectly reasonable answers.

2.   Ask your interviewer how long they have been with the company.

•   Their history can be very eye-opening, as you are trying to find out how happy they are with the culture. Their own experience can tell you a lot about growth opportunities.

3.   Ask how your interviewer would describe the organization's culture.

•   Get right to the point. I once asked this during an interview and was told, "The benefits are really good." That was all, no more no less, just that they liked the benefits. Hmmm, not exactly a resounding reason to join that team.

4.   What traits will the successful candidate possess?

- Pay close attention to the answer and then work their replies into your interview. For instance, if they say organizational skills. Provide them with an example of how you organize your workflow and goals. Your immediate goal is to move on to the next step.

5. Some general questions specific to event planning include:

   a. How are locations selected, who makes the final decision?

      - This will tell you how seriously they take site inspections and how much of the decision-making process you will own.

   b. How are speakers selected? How are they communicated with?

      - You want to know how much creative control you will have. Will you and your team have the ability to communicate with talent directly? Or will you be playing middleman because only an executive-level individual is significant enough to speak to talent?

   c. Who is responsible for agenda creation?

      - Just how many cooks are in that kitchen?

   d. How contracting venues are handled, who makes those decisions, and how far out are you contracted?

      - Do they use a 3rd party to source negotiations, or will this be on you?

    e.   How do you currently capture ROI?

- Do they have goals and standards? Or can you introduce these?

    f.   What type of professional development benefits do they offer?

- Will they support additional education and training?

Asking smart questions will tell you a lot about the company and help you decide if you want to continue with the interview. Once you make it past the hiring manager and are invited back, they are just sizing you up to see if you are someone they want to work with in the long run. Be upbeat, charming, and sincere in your approach.

I worked with a young woman who hated the interview process. She came across as cold and distant because she often let her nerves get the better of her. I encouraged her to take a different approach.

"Instead of looking at it as if this person is sizing you up for a dream job, think of them as a radio host or magazine journalist," I stated. "Think of them as being so interested in your background and success that they are doing a story on you." This technique seemed to help her in her job search, so I encourage you to look at them in the same way.

I will say it again, finding a new job is not easy. Especially one you just know you are going to be happy with. It is important to use your network (although, note that everyone is using their networks and maybe pulling on the same individuals) to cast a wide net. Use MPI, talk, and get involved.

It's so easy to say, "I'm not valued, I'm leaving." But it's another when you are out there sending out one awesome résumé after another and not even getting a bite on jobs a step or two below your skill set.

I want to make it clear I understand the guts it takes to make a change, but sticking around in a company, which doesn't respect you or your full potential and talent, is hurting you in ways you may not recognize. Just do yourself a favor and try to get out.

You must remain confident in your talent. You only get one round in this life, and you owe it to yourself to give yourself the best life you can while you are here. Even if you have to take a professional step backward, it just might be worth the departure to be happy. If a company fails to see your value or stops listening to you, then let them have the unschooled planner. Hopefully, then they will see the difference between a professional and a poser, and maybe then they will do themselves a favor and correct course before losing any more time, quality, and money.

Chapter 16:
Congratulations, you're a manager, now what?

You got the job, and because you are awesome, you have been promoted to manager! Good for you. You probably went out with some friends to celebrate your success and when you returned to work thought to yourself, "Oh crap. Now what?" Perfectly normal to feel that way. You were very good in your role, but now you are responsible for other people in their role. Yikes. So, now what?

Well, the good news is you have staff, a step in the right direction for our profession as we strive to be an independent department. That being said, managing event managers is damn difficult. These are professionals accustomed to being in charge and handling their agendas, vendors, contracted services, and teams.

The best advice I can give here is to give up the idea you manage any event professional. Remember, no one likes to be micromanaged. If they are truly a professional with the knowledge and skill to perform at the highest level, it's best to let them do their job.

Think of yourself as a talent manager working to get your clients noticed. Celebrate their wins and work with them to shine. If you have true event professionals on your team, acknowledge it and allow them to succeed by getting the hell out of their way.

That's not to say don't delegate, certainly you will need to assign tasks, but be very careful not to just toss the work you don't want to perform to them. Event professionals know the difference between quality projects and time-consuming tasks. If you delegate your dirty work, you won't be close to getting the best out of them. Give up thinking you know more than your staff because you are the boss. That is ludicrous, outdated thinking. You will need to strive to partner with your event professionals because you are all working for the same common goals, so do your best to align with your professionals. This will guarantee success.

Now, if you have unschooled planners on your team, that is another matter. With this group, you are going to have to work to nurture and educate them. Partner them with a more senior member of your staff and begin a mentor/mentee relationship. Give them lots of attention with weekly meetings to ask how they are doing, how they feel about the workload, what their goals are. Have candid conversations about ethics and encourage them to get involved in meeting planning associations. Although you will have to commit more time to these individuals, it's still important to point out that micromanagement is the destroyer of motivation, growth, and learning. It's an ugly method of poor leadership that is outdated and should be put out of its misery.

Now this is more difficult than said, but you must strive to treat all staff equally. Although you will have many different levels of experience and knowledge, it's important to embrace all team members, giving them the ability to truly contribute to the department. During brainstorming sessions, allow them the ability to toss up ideas, any ideas, and try to avoid letting them know why that won't work because you have more knowledge of the attendees, budget, and timing than they do. You never know when a great idea is going to be presented that will change the agenda for the better, so it's better just to keep an open mind.

I know that isn't always easy, but it's NOT ABOUT YOU. Once you move into a position where people report to you, it's no longer about your performance, so if you are someone who needs the spotlight, chocolate candies, and roses, do us all a favor and pass on the promotion.

I'm sure you have heard this before, but it's so true. A bad manager can take a good staff and destroy it, causing the best employees to flee and the remainder to lose all motivation. The best advice I ever received and the best advice I can give to managers is simply to think about all the times you were treated poorly by management. Now do the opposite.

I once had a boss who made it her first order of business to start having direct one-on-one meetings with my team. This was a while ago, but it still turns my stomach today. Yes, it is certainly her prerogative as my boss to do so, but if you are in a position where you happen to lead more than one layer of employees, please for the love of all that is good, do not do this. What you are essentially saying to your first-line employees is you do not trust them. And what you are saying to the second-tier employees is you are more important to their career than their direct manager. It ultimately caused a gap in team communication and overall trust. I often ask myself what the motivation was there, what was she hoping to gain by this?

Bad boss stories are as old as the pages they are written on. It's hard to understand why it's so darn easy to suck at leadership. Any suck-up can be given a leadership role, but it doesn't mean they are good at it. It's a serious problem costing companies millions annually.

Isn't it weird that employee surveys work one way? The manager can critique the employee and judge their work performance. Why are workers not asked to critique the style of management and treatment they endure from their boss? Imagine how productive that one action would be if managers were expected to receive a certain score to keep their leadership role year over year.

Although it's not required, I would encourage you as a leader to employ some type of survey for your staff to complete discreetly. I also encourage you to hold yourself accountable for how you treat your staff. Every leader should have a company goal included in their evaluation measuring their effectiveness as such.

It's not a coincidence that after the Covid-19 pandemic, a survey revealed a majority of the workforce had no interest in returning to an office environment. It wasn't just because they didn't have to dress in the morning or commute to work, it was due in large part to direct access with the boss. Professionals across the world have united in one honest statement: the less interaction with the boss, the more empowered they feel to do their job.

The bottom line here is if you are in a position of leadership, whether digital, in-person, hybrid, or hologram, for the love of all that is good, DO NOT micromanage, simply lead. Lead with trust, respect, empathy, and fairness. I can guarantee you and your employees will not only be happier but much more productive.

Chapter 17: Rinse, wash, repeat, and pay it forward

Now it is up to you. This is a long-haul process and one you will need to continue as you manage the road to the C-suite. The industry has done its part and taken us as far as it possibly can, but it cannot do it for us. It has tried. Aside from grabbing every CEO across the globe and strapping them to a chair via Clockwork Orange, we have been unable to reach the C-suite's ear to prove our value and worth to the organization as a professional planners. I hate to say it, guys, but it is up to us. It's time for a grassroots effort on our part to get loud, to knock on the C-suite door, and let them know over and over we are critical to the success of not only the events but the company as well.

The steps outlined in this book need to be practiced daily. We must hold ourselves to a higher standard than our HR, legal, Marketing, etc. department friends. The only way we are going to change the face of our industry and obtain the respect we deserve is by consistently showing our worth.

As part of our mission, I challenge each of you to pay it forward. If you are in a C-suite position, it is your responsibility to mentor your staff not only to succeed but to bring the skills and knowledge you have to other companies and roles. It is up to you to course correct the unschooled planners, to work with them on their professionalism and ethics. Create career paths for your staff, support their education, training, and task them with creating post-event reports. Challenge them to present at the next executive meeting. Share your story of success and how you achieved the seat at the table.

If you have not yet made it to the C-suite, then refer to Chapter 8 and start walking the walk. In addition, get involved with our industry associations, subscribe to publications, and make time to read them. Share your findings and please be professional in all things. Accept the feedback, change what you can. Get excited about the future of events and start talking to your leadership about virtual and hybrid and what that could look like long-term. Remain current and, for the love of all that is good, label your events appropriately. Know the difference between a workshop and a symposium.

It's up to us, but there is a lot of good in that. As long as we unite and do our part on the ground floor to establish our profession in each and every company where we work, it won't be long before we are viewed as a profession worthy of the C-suite. It is time to approach the locked door, get out our trusty picklock kit, and walk in confidently to take our seat at the table. Where, let's face it, we deserve to be.

A note from the Author:

—————————

I sincerely hope you enjoyed this book. I am passionate about this industry and as a result started All Access Coaching & Consulting. My handpicked team of event professionals and I are committed to helping you achieve your goals. Whether you are an individual looking for career advice and advancement or a business owner who is looking to form a world class event professional team, we are here to help you. Our industry is unique and presents specific and unique obstacles and challenges and it's because of that that I have designed a specific career and consulting firm, one that is laser focused on our profession.

Our individual coaching program is not your typical cooking cutter one size fits all coaching. The program we design together will be all about you. Your goals, your schedule, and most importantly your desired outcome. Whether you are looking for advancement or just want to talk through an opportunity, the team at All Access Coaching and Consulting are industry professionals that pride ourselves on designing solutions that focus on what motivates you. Together we will propel your strengths, achieve your goals, and shape your future as you define it to be.

Our consulting programs get to the heart of your companies needs. Whether your goals include tracking ROI, increasing attendee engagement, or leveraging all meeting platforms, we are here to help. We will work on defining your goals and collaborate with your existing staff on real concrete solutions that fit comfortably within your companies' values. From designing ethics and perks programs, to constructing reporting measures that work for your executive team, we will design solutions that will set you up for immediate and long-term continued success.

If you want to take control of your career and or event planning team, you are willing to put in the work, and you like the idea of learning from event professionals who has a proven body of success, then visit us at www.allaccesscoachingandconsulting. com to learn more about our team and services to get started on your success journey today.

Thank you for reading, and best of luck on the road to achieving all access.

Meeting Planning Resources:

MPI Academy, CMP Master Class

Meeting Professionals International

Events Industry Council

www.allaccesscoachingandconsulting.com

Publications list:

PCMA Convene

Meetings Today

Associations Now

Bisbash

MeetingsNet

Meetings & Conventions

Event Marketer